Copyright © 2020

Printed in the United States of America

All rights reserved to the Author. No part of this publication may be reproduced, distributed, or transmitted in any form or by any means, including photocopying, recording, or other electronic or mechanical methods, without the prior written permission of the publisher, except in the case of brief quotations embodied in critical reviews and commercial uses permitted by copyright law. For permission requests, write to the publisher, addressed "Attention: Permissions Coordinator," at the address below.

ISBN: 978-1-7350262-0-6   (Paperback)
ISBN: 978-1-7350262-1-3   (Ebook)

Any references to historical events, real people, or real places are used fictitiously. Names, characters, and places are products of the author's imagination and experiences.

Biblical context and quotation is taken from King James Version and New Living Translation

Front cover by Author Meek "Klassi Ladi" Miles

Publishing Company: GroundWorks Management LLC
P.O. Box 241225
Chicago IL, 60624

Business Email: groundworksmgmtllc@gmail.com
Strike A Match Email: strikeamatch07@gmail.com

Strike A Match

A 60-day Devotional to Heal, Build, & Reveal God's Purpose

Strike A Match is a network of men and women who thirst after God's direction for their lives. Its a Lifestyle brand that empower others to ignite the flame in creating successful relationships, families, and businesses. After getting caught up in the entrapments of the world, and falling prey to everyday mistakes; we realized the need to reprogram our thinking and develop positive decision making skills. While life happens to all of us, it was easier to blame others than acknowledge that we didn't know it all, or refuse to obey the principles of God's Word, than to be in alignment with who we are destined to be. It's true, none of us are greater than the other, and most of us if we're honest can relate to the pain, guilt, shame, and brokenness so common in our culture. To admit we need help, oh that takes a level of courage very few have, and to combat such trauma with tools that don't involve self-medication is almost unheard. The lack of Mental Health awareness is one of many silent killers in the world today, and even more prevalent in the Black community. Most blacks can relate to growing up with family members who suffered from mental illness that was triggered by a real problem; molestation, alcoholism, substance abuse, incarceration, poverty, and grief. And while it was easier to categorize that person as "crazy" or deny the signs of destruction; adequate time and resources were never a priority. This devotional was written to help combat those negative apprehensions and responses we've developed; in hopes that we heal from our past, celebrate our future, and restore God's Divine Purpose through Testimony.

Copyright: © 2020
Publishing: GroundWorks Management LLC

Strike A Match Ent. "Igniting the Flame to Purpose, Passion, and Empowerment."

Dedication & Acknowledgment

Blessings to My Kings and Queens:

I wanted to dedicate this book to my Heavenly Father, Yahweh you are my fortress and refuge. You are a father and friend, there is none like you. When I need you most, you are there; when I think of joy I think of you. The turn of events in my life would have sent your strongest warrior into a downward spiral, but you have kept me and caused me to Rise above. Because you revealed your word to me and placed your commandments on my heart, I now walk in Purpose and Truth. I am forever grateful for you, the True and Living God.

Secondly, I would like to acknowledge and thank my mother for her strength, for setting such a wonderful example. Dina, you are my queen, and if I am half the woman you are, then I know I'll make it to Heaven with glass slippers on. Thank you for your support and encouragement, every step of the way.
I thank my Earthly father, who may not be with me in the natural, but always in the Spirit. My angel, you raised me to be tough, to work hard and hustle smart; you taught me what a REAL man is supposed to be. And every promise I made to you before your last breath, Yah's will it shall come to pass. I also want to acknowledge and dedicate this book to my Sun, my rider, my favorite young King in the whole world. I gave birth to you, and in return you developed me into a Woman. You made me a MOM, a woman who craved more out of life, a woman who believed the mysteries of Yah would be our treasure chest to live our best life. We grew up together, we learn together, and we'll forever be God's prized possession. I love you young man, keep reaching for the stars cause the World is yours.

Lastly, but just as important, I acknowledge and dedicate this book to the one who holds my Heart and carry the Crown. You came into my life while I was hidden in Christ, doing the work of my Father, and tending to my garden. Our vibe was real, our stories collided, and our Spirits danced. It was true, Heaven had gifted me with my Purpose Partner, and I am honored to share this life with you. I pray that all of our dreams come true, all of our memories are magical, and all of our desires prosper. This is only the beginning, JHamp, let's go strike while it's hot; and blaze a trail of our own. Kingdom Building!!

To all of my family and friends, I love you, I thank you for your support, I value each of you, and I am forever grateful for all that you pour into me. Follow your dreams, beat the odds, and remain humble. Trust your process and know that what God has for you, it is for you. No matter what you have gone through, no matter who didn't like it, and no matter how many times you fall, the only way to the top is forward. Peace be unto you.

                                              Love,

                                                  Klassi Ladi
                                                  "Meek"

God's Love Draws Near

Blessings to My Kings and Queens:

So one of the most valuable lessons we can take away from King Solomon and Queen Sheba's encounter is that Solomon's favor drew others closer to God. Traveling from afar and bringing gifts to your Highness, Queen of Sheba was so amazed by the wisdom, royal leadership, and power of King Solomon that she asked questions, sought advice, gained companionship, and insight from the Lord. She recognized how blessed Solomon was, his servants honored him, he was prosperous and well respected, he was humble and of good morale. His ability to teach her and be vulnerable in honesty was commendable; it was unheard of amongst Rulers. Have you ever met someone that sparked your interest simply from the Glory of God that shined upon them. Like you were so intrigued to know more about the level of maturity and wisdom they spoke from, the level of excellence and authority they worked from, and their level of execution in compassion. It caused you to go seek the Kingdom, find peace and identity in truth, and begin to move more like Christ. Has love reminded you of the goodness and mercy of God? Have you ever wanted more for yourself and someone else, to the extent, you sought God's wisdom on how to build together, how to grow together, and how to live in search of Purpose; even if it meant being real with them about your flaws, doing the work necessary to not bring pain and hurt their way, or respecting the boundaries of relationship.

This is my prayer for you: Heavenly Father we come in agreement and ask for godly connections filled with your Spirit and power. No longer will we cling to brokenness, unstable relationships, irresponsible behavior, and generational trauma. We will seek your face and obey your Word for all understanding, we will imitate your mature wisdom for that which we do not know. We will not repeat the cycles of infidelity, abuse, and selfish intent. Instead Lord, let our hearts be filled with your gracious love so that we can pour into others, what you have kindly given us. We shall Love and Honor one another!

In Yeshua's name Amen

1 Kings 10

The Queen of Sheba Visits Solomon

When the queen of Sheba heard about the fame of Solomon and his relationship to the Lord, she came to test Solomon with hard questions. Arriving at Jerusalem with a very great caravan—with camels carrying spices, large quantities of gold, and precious stones—she came to Solomon and talked with him about all that she had on her mind. Solomon answered all her questions; nothing was too hard for the king to explain to her. When the queen of Sheba saw all the wisdom of Solomon and the palace he had built, the food on his table, the seating of his official, the attending servants in their robes, his cupbearers, and the burnt offerings he made at the temple of the Lord, she was overwhelmed.

She said to the king, "The report I heard in my own country about your achievements and your wisdom is true. But I did not believe these things until I came and saw with my own eyes. Indeed, not even half was told me; in wisdom and wealth you have far exceeded the report I heard. How happy your people must be! How happy your officials, who continually stand before you and hear your wisdom! Praise be to the Lord your God, who has delighted in you and placed you on the throne of Israel. Because of the Lord's eternal love for Israel, he has made you king to maintain justice and righteousness."

**Self Reflection: What has love INSPIRED you to do?

_____
_____
_____
_____
_____
_____
_____
_____
_____
_____
_____
_____

Cop Anxiety

Blessings to my Kings and Queens:

Some of us are way too familiar with the rush of anxiety that overtakes us when a cop pulls behind our vehicle. Even when you know you haven't done anything wrong, you're obeying the speed limit and all of a sudden you switch lanes to avoid them. Now you're turning off the road and getting further away from your destination. Paranoid and in a state of panic, this is how we address problems in our life, the first sign of trouble and we forget to be courageous and stand firm on Yah's word. We begin to contemplate Plan B and C, coming up with our own scenarios of defeat, we lose sight of the command Yahweh told us in the beginning; the fact that Christ overcame the world and so will we. "Do not be afraid for He is with you, do not grow weary in long suffering, trust that He has gone before you and made your crooked path straight." One of the greatest things to know is that Yah is pleased with our Faithfulness, He rewards us for staying the course and not growing anxious. When we've experienced trauma and heartache, of any sort; we begin to have PTSD and unhealthy coping skills of flight or fight. We deal with things differently and begin to react to others, based on the way we were treated in the past, or out of our inability to heal first. The pressures of what we've been through begins to take root in our hearts and minds, and cause us to fear being hurt again, panic when we see similar signs, or become obsessed with never feeling that way again. And what the latter does is prevent you from ever forgiving; the longer you ponder the way it made you feel, the less likely you are to move forward. We hold on to these experiences and babysit the pain it caused, nursing our insecurities in dysfunction. I know way too many people who have made the excuse, "This just how I am" "I don't believe in that" "Life made me this way" "He/She made me a savage" "I don't trust anyone" "I'll never let someone do me like that again." The trauma of broken families, situationships, years of oppression, police brutality, and lack of self-awareness, have caused us anxiety, attachment issues, disassociation, anger, resentment, and a lot of self-loathing. We use these general statements or nonchalant reactions to overcompensate and hide behind a mask of conflict or refusal to change. Instead, take deep breaths, weigh your options, heal from the things that hurt you, and have faith in what is to come. This should be done daily!

Joshua 1:8 "Do not let this Book of the Law depart from your mouth; meditate on it day and night, so that you may be careful to do everything written in it. Then you will be prosperous and successful."

Philippians 4:6-7 "Do not be anxious about anything, but in everything by prayer and supplication with thanksgiving let your requests be made known to God."

 Isaiah 43:1 "But now, this is what the Lord says…Fear not, for I have redeemed you; I have summoned you by name; you are mine."

Psalm 23:4 "Even though I walk through the valley of the shadow of death, I will fear no evil, for you are with me; your rod and your staff, they comfort me."

**Self Reflection: What causes your anxiety, what triggers you to be anxious or weary? And what helps to calm your nerve when confronted with unfamiliar pressure?
TAKE DEEP BREATHS AND MEDITATE BEFORE ANSWERING

_____
_____
_____
_____
_____
_____
_____
_____
_____
_____
_____
_____
_____
_____
_____
_____
_____
_____
_____
_____

Stop Shoppin' on E

Blessings to My Kings and Queens:

Why is that every time I go to the grocery store while I'm hungry, I end up purchasing everything. Literally going down aisles, I normally wouldn't and putting everything in the cart that I could imagine cooking. In my head, I'm meal prepping and planning cook-outs for the family, creating this illusion. Oh and don't let there be an item on sale, five for ten, give me that...Buy one get one free, oh that too.
Shopping on an empty stomach will have you making unnecessary purchases and thinking you're getting a deal even when you're not. Without a grocery list of items, sizing up your cupboard with what you need to replace, and sticking to the plan; you'll find yourself easily persuaded.

Hebrews 13:21 says

He will Equip you with everything good that you may do his will, working in us that which is pleasing in his sight, through Jesus Christ, to whom be glory forever and ever. Amen.

Allow the holy Spirit to fill you up and equip you with the wisdom, knowledge, and understanding to maintain and elevate a marriage. Date with purpose not with passion, because an empty stomach will settle for anything, or be full on that which it cannot handle. Wholeness is the goal before Oneness of two Souls. So consider this same philosophy of truth in all areas of your life.Have a plan, set boundaries and parameters of what you will and will not accept, stick to the G-Code of God's word, and never do anything out of desperation. Shopping on E, will have you selling your birthrights for a meal, just like Esau. In the Book of Genesis, Chapter 25:29-34, Esau came in the house from the field and was sooo hungry that when he saw Jacob cooking stew, he asked for some and stated he'd be willing to sell his birthright, the inheritance of his namesake. "What good will it be, if I died from starvation." How many of us can relate, in a world of thirst trap and hungry savages, we'd be willing to sell our souls for a quick meal or dollar. Something that is ours from birth, spoken over us before the formation of the Earth, that the Lord breathe life into us for hope and a future; and here it is, we risk it all for instant gratification. We don't want to wait for the future part, the manifestation of His plan and timing; so we settle for the money, fame, and lifestyle of Esau. Giving up everything we are entitled to, in desperation of lies, deceit, immorality, over-saturated success, tasteless character, and reckless curses. Of course we don't necessarily see it that way, because it appears to be everything we want in that moment; like my experience in the grocery store, so many options and possibilities, we just gotta have it. Being on E (empty), causes us to seek satisfaction. Our innate instinct is to satisfy that craving or desire because our bodies have not been trained to seek God first. Which is why, the Lord saw fit to remind us, "seek ye the Kingdom first, and everything else will be added unto you." When we make the conscious decision to seek God first, we can then assess what He want for us and have to give us. We'll begin to decipher what is good and what is not, what is worth our time and what is wasting our time, what is blessing us and what is hurting us, what we should take hold and what should be left on the shelf. Creating a list, taking inventory and making the best use of what you have, blocking out the distractions of what does not serve you well, allows you to shop (live) with purpose and intention. It prevents you from selling out, giving in, or losing the blessings our Lord and Saviour has already promised.

**Self Reflection: What is it that you have sold, lost, or given up in desperation?

_____
_____
_____
_____
_____
_____
_____
_____
_____
_____
_____
_____
_____
_____
_____
_____
_____
_____
_____

Your Plan, His Will

Blessings to My Kings and Queens:

When we focus on our goals and get serious about manifesting our dreams, the universe has a way of sending distractions and roadblocks to hinder elevation; but please remember the word of God warned us of the perils that come. Stay planted, stay focused, and remain in the Will of God; for all things work together for the good of those who love the Lord. We are reminded that it's not about the destination, but more so the journey. Jesus himself was detoured several times, leaving Nazareth when the people were not ready to receive His word, or having to face off with the enemy for 40 days, Paul was sent to prison and still confessed the Gospel, and Joshua had battle after battle to take hold of the Promise land. Let these stories be examples of staying the course and trusting God's plan, regardless of how the plan changes. Jehovah Jireh is our Provider, the Lord of Provisions, will make a way out of no way. Even when we have a plan, and have double checked the when, where, and how; He will still step in and do what He sees fit. Our Lord knows us better than we know ourselves, and with that being said, there are times we have a plan or goal, and God disrupts it because He knows that #1. We are not ready, #2. It is not in our best interest, #3. It will derail us in the future, #4. He has something better, or #5. It is not the right time. But in the midst of the Lord working, the enemy will try to stick his hand in the business too.

And his only weapon of attack is to divide and conquer, so he'll distract you with unproductive options, he'll send temporary success, or he'll interrupt your plans so that you no longer believe that it can and will happen for you. You'll begin to encounter rejection, doubt, fear, and sometimes uneasiness about doing something new. However, if you will remain connected to the Vine, the Lord of Lords and King of Kings, you'll produce great fruit, you'll achieve your goals, and His will shall be done.

Isaiah 54: 17 says, "No weapon formed against you shall prosper, And every tongue which rises against you in judgment You shall condemn. This is the heritage of the servants of the LORD, And their righteousness is from Me," Says the LORD.

Your inheritance is from the Most High, so there is no weapon that will prosper against you, and God has a way of making even the mistakes and stumbling blocks work for your good. The traps of the enemy will be a building block and not a stronghold, the detour will be a pit stop and not the end of your road. Learn to fight with the Word of God and speak against that which tries to attack you, keep a scripture in your heart and on your lips, for the very moments someone try to hinder your movement, even if its yourself.

**Self Reflection: What is my Plan and What is God's Will for my life? How can I make the two align?

_____
_____
_____
_____
_____
_____
_____
_____
_____
_____
_____
_____
_____
_____
_____
_____
_____
_____
_____
_____
_____
_____
_____

Bit the Apple Pt. 1

Blessings to My Kings and Queens:

Who told you that?... Some of us are holding on to the comments of the enemy, making His word the Law of Life. We govern ourselves and move according to what "they" said we couldn't do or be. Now the inner voices in your own head are holding you back from starting the business, going for the new position, taking the trip, asking that woman out, setting demands on the relationship, confronting those abandonment issues, or lying to yourself about rejection. This is how "they" operate. People who are too afraid to do what it is you're trying to do, or so small minded that they will kill big dreams. Some of us know loved ones, family members, and friends who speak against everything you believe or wish to do, simply because its too hard for them, or have never been done. In order to combat the joy stealers, dream killers, doubt seekers, we must remember what was "So" from the beginning of time. Remember the truth and not the lies; because the moment you taste the words of doubt, you'll begin to create the appetite for it. Stop eating and digesting the fruit of evil that causes you to regurgitate the lies and deceit of the enemy because God gave you the fruit of life and knowledge. Genesis 3:11 says, And God said, "Who told you that you were naked? Have you eaten from the tree of which I commanded you that you should not eat?" Then the man said, "The woman whom You gave to be with me, she gave me of the tree, and I ate." And the Lord God said to the woman, "What is this you have done?" The woman said, "The serpent deceived me, and I ate." We all know this story, when the Serpent deceived Eve into biting the apple, and she gave some to Adom (spelled this way, purposely). After biting the apple, man and woman were now open to good and evil, knowledge and sin; their eyes were open, to their nakedness. Just because someone offers you their opinion, their reality, their beliefs, doesn't mean you have to accept. We don't have to eat from the plate of Judas, who handed Jesus over to the Pharisees to be killed (John 18:3-13); nor do we have to eat from the tree of disbelief, rotten fear, and insecurity. Be conscious of The Who, that you allow in your head, and be exposed to your ideas and goals. Be careful of who's speaking life and death into you, who's reacting to your discomfort and who's building your confidence. Especially when some people are willing to feed you that which is not good for you, to open your eyes and see all of the things you cannot do or be. Instead share in the appetite of healthy believers, individuals who bear good fruit, who helps you see the possibilities of wholeness. Let go of the naysayers who make buffet plates of cold hearted lies, hot mess desserts, and lukewarm support. "They" don't want to see you win, "They" do not believe in themselves, so how can they believe in you.

John 12: 36-38
"While you have the Light, believe in the Light, so that you may become sons of light." After Jesus had spoken these things, He went away and was hidden from them. Although Jesus had performed so many signs in their presence, they still did not believe in Him. This was to fulfill the word of Isaiah the prophet: "Lord, who has believed our message? And to whom has the arm of the Lord been revealed?"…

Selah and Amen

**Self Reflection: Create two Lists of Names

Who in my life Believes in Me?

_____

_____

_____

_____

_____

Who in my life does not Believe in Me?

_____

_____

_____

_____

_____

Bit the Apple Pt.2

Blessings to My Kings and Queens:

Before the Taste of Evil there was nothing you couldn't do, you were dominant, brave, fruitful, courageous, and you believed in yourself. What is it gonna take to get your courage back, to get back to the place where you did exactly what you set out to; you didn't procrastinate, you didn't wait for your parents, you weren't looking for likes and validation. As a matter of fact, you didn't even have the credentials to do it, you weren't a pro in none of the areas you stepped into; but with your brave heart and faith, you swam in deep waters, you leaped and found out you had wings to fly. Remember growing up, and believing in yourself; trying out for the sports team little league, performing at talent shows even though you never had professional training, starting your own social clubs amongst friends, being an entrepreneur selling candy in school. Whatever it was you wanted to do, you made a plan and executed; there wasn't time to second guess or consider "what paperwork do I need" "what are my friends gonna think" "what certifications must I have" "how many likes can I get." Let's get back to that place, let's reignite the flame that burned inside of you. The flame that wouldn't let you rest until things got done, wouldn't let you give up until you saw the manifestation of what you believed, wouldn't let you slip until you took hold of what you wanted. In a world with so many look-a likes, culture vultures, and repeat offenders; be not afraid to stand out. Be different, be set apart, be unique, be You. None of us have the same design, and **Psalm 139: 13-18** reminds us that Yah created our innermost parts, fearfully and wonderfully as

He wanted. With knowing that, we can stand bold and be daring in our works. We can be audacious in our approach and hustle; because of whose we are, because of the power and authority we walk in, and because of the anointing over our lives. Way back when, before the nay-sayers and before we became consumed with what others thought about us; we were lionhearted, we were unafraid to try new things and take risks. We were willing to follow the original command given in the Garden of Eden; Be fruitful, multiply, have dominion over the earth. And in a season of possessing what is yours, we have to regain that Joshua spirit, we have to be relentless like David, and fearless like Esther.

Ezekiel 28:13-19

"You were in Eden, the garden of God; Every precious stone was your covering: The ruby, the topaz and the diamond; The beryl, the onyx and the jasper; The lapis lazuli, the turquoise and the emerald; And the gold, the workmanship of your settings and sockets, Was in you. On the day that you were created They were prepared. "You were the anointed cherub who covers, And I placed you there You were on the holy mountain of God; You walked in the midst of the stones of fire. "You were blameless in your ways From the day you were created Until unrighteousness was found in you.

With Love,

    Klassi

Self Reflection: I am not afraid to….

_____
_____
_____
_____
_____
_____
_____
_____
_____
_____
_____
_____
_____
_____
_____
_____
_____
_____
_____

Trust the Process

Blessings to My Kings and Queens:

There will be some valley moments that test your faith and strength in the Lord. But also to humble you and prepare you for greater. And if you don't sustain and keep your eyes on what the Lord has promised, you'll lose sight and get caught up in growing pains. Growing pains occur when we're elevating from Glory to Glory; going from one level of understanding to the next, and maturing in our experiences of everyday life. In order to be moved in wisdom, we have to learn from our mistakes, pass the test, and use what we've learned in application. I want to encourage you during those valley moments, the moments that are part of the training, that breaks and mold you into being a better servant of Yah. It teaches you to lean not on your own understanding, conditions you to be at peace and work hard for what your heart desire, those moments show you how to deal with others, and survive hard times. If you continue to trust the Lord during the dark season, you'll be better equipped to maintain the blessing on the Mountaintop. I know it seems to be too much, and you don't believe He's listening to your prayers sometimes, but He is. When things start falling apart, we don't realize that on the flip side, something else is coming together. And He cannot give you what you are yet to take hold; because it will be a waste to let it slip through your fingers due to arrogance, self pride, lack of skill, and evil intentions. Can you imagine that, losing the very thing you've always wanted because you were too arrogant to appreciate it, or stubborn to compromise for it, or too immature to understand what it takes to maintain. In the words of Prophet Tupac Shakur, "I'm not saying I'm gonna change the world, but I guarantee that I will spark the brain that will." We have to trust that whatever part we play, whatever decisions we make, and whatever trial we endure; it will all be for the good, and eventually lend towards the progression of a people. Let the love of our Heavenly Father prepare you in His timing. God's timing allows us to pause when we need to, move when we have to, and increase our awareness of what season we're in. And trusting that process, assures us that the proper training and skills we gain during this time, will help us be successful, prosperous, and walking in abundance.

Isaiah 54:10

"For the mountains may depart and the hills be removed, but my steadfast love shall not depart from you, and my covenant of peace shall not be removed," says the Lord, who has compassion on you.

Psalm 112:7

"He is not afraid of bad news; his heart is firm, trusting the Lord."

Ecclesiastes 3:1

"There is a time for everything, and a season for every activity under the heavens"

Self Reflection: What am I to learn in this season?

DreamChasers

Blessings to My Kings and Queens:

In the book of Genesis, Joseph told a dream to his brothers about visions he had foreseen. He didn't know that it would be his meal ticket to a life of ups & downs, as they didn't agree with what he spoke. Joseph was sold off and hated for the revelation of his vision, and experienced prison, slavery, and abuse. However, he did not focus on the challenges thrown at him, nor did he allow them to harden his heart or lose sight of the original dream. Somehow, God still brought it to pass after a life of tests and trials, Joseph was a blessed man who was given dominion over Egypt. And just as it was written, Joseph's brothers had to bow down to him, and reap a harvest of crop and grain. After selling their brother and lying to their father Jacob, that Joseph died; Joseph was later sent to prison on the account of Potiphar's wife who lied about him trying to seduce her. His ability to interpret dreams and prophecy the meaning of dreams, Joseph gain favor in prison and eventually with Pharaoh. Just when the moment presented itself, Joseph was called to the palace to interpret Pharaoh's dream. In preparation of a famine, Joseph was given authority to govern over the land and grain. He was responsible for helping the people survive, including his own family, who failed to believe him in previous time. How is it, when test and trial come, some of us forget the original plan and dream we had because of the difficult circumstances we endure. But I want you to awaken the dream and keep your mind set on that which was revealed. Eat, sleep, and breathe your dream so that it will become a reality; the process along the way is just a set of events destined to help you get there. So even when it doesn't look like its going to happen, when things do not appear as it should be, and other people try to discredit the vision; keep your eyes and heart inclined to the Lord. Those dreams are like trailers to a movie, a preview of what's to come. God doesn't give the full play by play, He doesn't make known the turn of events that will occur prior to the expected end. Similar to the prophecy given to Mary, as the Mother of the Messiah, she didn't know her son would be crucified. The children of Israel didn't know that they would survive slavery, crossing a Red Sea, famine, and battle to possess the Promise Land. Paul didn't know that he would go from persecuting and killing Believers, to becoming a Servant of Christ. And Job didn't know he would have to endure death of family, lost of inheritance, sickness, and bankruptcy before receiving a double portion of God's blessings. Remember these things as you press toward the mark, chase your dream and see it come to pass. Though it is given in part, and only God knows the detail, Meek Mill said it best " yo grind will turn into yo shine...keep Forrest Gumpin"

Genesis 37:5-7
Joseph had a dream, and when he told it to his brothers, they hated him all the more. He said to them, "Listen to this dream I had: We were binding sheaves of grain out in the field when suddenly my sheaf rose and stood upright, while your sheaves gathered around mine and bowed down to it."

Joel 2:28
"And it shall come to pass afterward, that I pour out my Spirit on all flesh; your sons and your daughters shall prophesy, your old men shall dream dreams, and your young men shall have visions."

**Self Reflection: The dream I'm chasing is….

Time to Celebrate!

Blessings to My Kings and Queens:

Yesssss...we did that! In the name of Yeshua Hamashiach (Jesus Christ) we proclaim victory over this last season. Victory over this last test! Victory over this last experience! The countdown begins, and as we look over the many obstacles and tests that were thrown at us, we can praise His Holy name. Give yourself a hand, and delight in the sweet taste of Victory, for your Lord and Saviour came through, just as He promised. There were times you wanted to give up, moments that confused you, tried to knock you down, and test your Faith. But God in all His righteousness, His unfailing love for you, continued to push you higher. Way above the hand of the enemy, way above the naysayers, way above the traps of defeat. While this season, no matter how long it seemed, was full of great preparation, it has positioned you right where God wants you to be. With clear vision and a surrendered heart, let's shout for joy that His plan is always greater than our own. Cheers to you for doing the work necessary to renew your mind, heal your heart, and submit to His perfect will. It only gets greater from here your highness...join the ranks of your sisters and brothers; here's to a crown of royal priesthood! The flame is ignited and the trail is lit. There is a healthier, more responsible way to celebrate than to sit around drinking and smoking, or going to the club and wasting money, or doing something dangerous for a thrill. YOLO moments do not have to be life threatening, or full of extreme circumstances with unfavorable consequences on the back end. There are productive ways to turn up; try traveling the world, hosting a launch party, cutting the ribbon to a new business venture, giving back to the community, creating memories with family, and elevating your level of pleasure. Celebrations in the black community are in dire need of a re-vamp, some of us have to go back to the drawing board and re-consider what we equate joy and fulfillment to be. Having a good time and celebrating moments of accomplishment, should not end a tragedy, heated disagreements, unproductive discourse, or drama-filled propaganda. We have to learn to keep the mood lighthearted, respectful, and memorable; all for the Glory of God.

Genesis 50:20

"As for you, you meant evil against me, but God meant it for good in order to bring about this present result, to preserve many people alive.

Exodus 23:20-23

"Behold, I am going to send an angel before you to guard you along the way and to bring you into the place which I have prepared. "Be on your guard before him and obey his voice; do not be rebellious toward him, for he will not pardon your transgression, since My name is in him. "But if you truly obey his voice and do all that I say, then I will be an enemy to your enemies and an adversary to your adversaries.

Revelation 19:1-2

After these things I heard something like a loud voice of a great multitude in heaven, saying, "Hallelujah! Salvation and glory and power belong to our God; BECAUSE HIS JUDGMENTS ARE TRUE AND RIGHTEOUS; for He has judged the great harlot who was corrupting the earth with her immorality, and HE HAS AVENGED THE BLOOD OF HIS SERVANTS!

**Self Reflection: What has God brought you from? How have you grown?

_____
_____
_____
_____
_____
_____
_____
_____
_____
_____
_____
_____
_____
_____
_____
_____
_____

Love Thy Neighbors as Thyself

Blessings to My Kings and Queens:

As a true believer, neighbor, and friend we must consider the importance of supporting each other through our difficulties. If my friend has a habit of smoking and they are trying to stop I shouldn't smoke around them, or try to pass my choice of sin over to them; if they have a gambling habit why will I invite them to the casino? If my sister has been struggling with promiscuity or lustful desires we are not gonna spend time discussing sexcapades or hanging out with random men, I'm not going to celebrate her decision to continue to fall short. It's one thing to help a person acknowledge their faults, and another to contribute to their sins. The bible says it would be better for us to lose an eye if it causes us to fall into temptation. Or if what you eat, "causes your brother to fall in sin, you should never eat meat again so you won't cause them to fall." What are you "eating" or digesting mentally, physically, and spiritually that causes someone else to go astray? How important is it to have godly friendships and encounters that consider the well-being of someone else. Having the kind of goals that truly honor and love others as you love yourself. Loving a neighbor teaches us to be accountable for what we do and how we present ourselves to God, because He will judge us for our choices and decisions. Even if it causes harm to another, or send them into the traps of the enemy, whether that's sexual immorality, adultery, pornography, deceit, theft, slander, or murder. There are so many things that we partake in and don't realize that it causes another person to fall short, or adapt in transgression. Your language becomes their language, your choices become their choices, their sin becomes your sin; as the word says bad company corrupts moral character (1 Corinthians 15:33). That is why scripture reiterated the importance of loving our neighbor as we love ourselves, because the Lord knows what it mean to care for someone else. To show compassion and kindness to our brothers and sisters, to see our neighbor as we see ourselves in truth and loyalty. Think about the gang culture; a group of individuals who are connected in the struggle of brokenness, they share the commonality of pain, hurt, lost, insecurity, sense of belonging. The very areas, the enemy can prey on are the very areas the Lord want to have total control. And through our friendships, relationships, association with others, God can heal those areas, He can cause new mercy and opportunity to make those dry areas breathe again, He can connect us with godly people who love and respect one another. The "gang" mentality have great qualities, when used in the context of righteousness; we can belong to a Kingdom, we can be secure in the relationships we build for the goodness of others, we can protect one another from stumbling, and confess our sins to finally gain closure and help one another heal from past experiences. The more that we align ourselves in this manner, the more we'll create healthy friendships, healthy families, healthy ministries, and healthy marriages. I love you, not because you have done something for me, but because the Bible tells me so!

Matthew 22:36-39

Master, which is the great commandment in the Law? Jesus said unto him, "Thou shalt love the Lord thy God with all thy heart, and with all thy soul, and with all thy mind. This is the first and great commandment. And the second is like unto it, Thou shalt love thy neighbor as thyself."

**Self Reflection: How can I be a better friend?

_____
_____
_____
_____
_____
_____
_____
_____
_____
_____
_____
_____

Holy Spirit

Blessings to My Kings and Queens:

When we endure different situations in life, we would normally call the first person we can and talk about what's goin on. We need someone to validate our frustration or agree with our reaction; not even to help us through. Well I've learned sometimes when we don't know how to handle a problem or see how to change it, it may be best to call on the Holy Spirit, instead of a random friend who'll give their opinion. Yah's word tells us to be filled with the Spirit that leads in all understanding, that gives us rest when things don't make sense, and gives us direction on how to move forward. The Holy Spirit teaches self control, discipline, regard for others, and patience. Not just to wait in fury, but to wait in expectation. There is freedom in the Spirit, to help us do what has never been done before. Even if that means breaking generational curses, changing careers, removing ourselves from toxic people, letting go of past hurt, not getting revenge on those that crossed us, or being content with where God has us. When we're going through something whether good or bad, the Holy Spirit comforts us and give confirmation on what to do. Especially when confiding in others, isn't always the easiest to do; everything is not for everybody. Some people out of their own insecurity, disbelief, or uncertainty, are unable to help you make sense or seek resolution on a problem. Have you ever called someone to tell them what you're going through, or just got news and you want to share; and they either make things worse by feeding you all of these what ifs, or they're unable to be genuinely happy for you. I've been there before, and during a season when no one could relate to what I was going through, I found peace and refuge in the Holy Spirit. Knowing that Jesus left a comforter, a guiding light, and fortitude to overcome anything, helps me to stand and not be moved from the Father's presence. When we accept Jesus (Yeshua) as our Lord and Saviour, the Spirit abide in us, the Spirit of the Lord is not something we put on and take off at our leisure, instead we become one with an advocate. As you arise daily, take time to ask the Lord to come into your life and make His abode there; clear your temple of all things toxic and evil, and allow God to make a sanctuary in the crevices of your heart.

John 14:16
"And I will ask the Father, and he will give you another advocate to help you and be with you forever."

2 Corinthians 3:17
"Now the Lord is the Spirit, and where the Spirit of the Lord is, there is freedom."

Self Reflection: Where in your life have you noticed the Holy Spirit? Have you experienced something outside of yourself, that you know only the Spirit of the Lord could have controlled or handled?

_____
_____
_____
_____
_____
_____
_____
_____
_____
_____
_____
_____
_____
_____
_____
_____
_____
_____
_____
_____

Changed Perspective

Blessings to My Kings and Queens:

Having a changed perspective and outlook is one of the hardest areas to transform, when we have been programmed to move, live, and be who we are currently. We have learned behavior, attitudes, and morals that fit our today, based on what we've experienced yesterday. You know the whole concept nature vs. nurture, we become a Product of our environment, knowingly and unknowingly. However, moving outside of the social constructs built around us will allow us to go further in life and be who we want to be, not who others say we are. So many of us limit our own capacity by wearing the banner of Ex-offender, single mother, college drop-out, dope boy, playa, side chick, because of past mistakes. We step into the box, "society" creates for us, and make it home instead of a temporary dwelling place. And now here we are living in the hotel of our situation too afraid to check out and move on. It becomes easier to blame the "label" and stereotype as to why we haven't progressed in life; than to say it's because we didn't apply ourselves, don't know how to move on, or we're comfortable being a lesser version of our true selves. But Jehovah Nissi, holds up a banner of Victory, and proclaims we have all sinned and fallen short of His grace. Which is why He sent His only begotten son, yet while we were sinners to pay the price for our transgressions. Praises be unto You Lord, for taking my flaws, taking my sins, taking my lies, taking my evil intentions, taking my lustful desires, taking my pride of self-serving agendas, and taking my past upon the cross, nailing them into the stakes of your hand, and washing them clean with your Blood. We can call things which are not, as though they are, and trust the blemishes of our past have been buried and raised with a New power, a New design, and New Purpose. Be transformed by the renewing of your mind and daily accept the banner of Victory that you have overcome, just as Christ our Brother has.

Romans 4:17
(as it is written: "I have made thee a father of many nations"), in the presence of Him whom he believed, even God, who quicken the dead and call those things which are not, as though they were.

2 Corinthians 4:17-18
"For our present troubles are small and won't last very long. Yet they produce for us a glory that vastly outweighs them and will last forever."

1 John 3:9
"No one born of God makes a practice of sinning, for God's seed (God's Elect) abide in Him, and he cannot keep on sinning because he has been born of God."

Self Reflection: You are no longer who you used to be, we have humbled ourselves, prayed, and began to seek the Face of the true and living Father, Yahweh. Your sin has been forgiven, and all has been healed in the name of the Lord. So what can you change about today? Who can you be today, because the former things have passed away!

_____
_____
_____
_____
_____
_____
_____
_____
_____
_____
_____
_____
_____
_____
_____
_____
_____
_____
_____
_____

Detox Often

Blessings to My Kings and Queens:

The definition of detox is a process or period of time in which one abstains from or rids the body of toxic unhealthy substances. It is important to rid our mind and body of the things that are toxic to our thoughts and behaviors, our fleshly desires of lust, insecurity, bad habits, selfish intentions, and disobedience. So learning to cleanse yourself from mental trauma, requires an understanding of prayer and meditation, fasting and fellowship with other believers, and surrounding yourself with humble like minded individuals. Can you imagine binge eating a lot of sweets, carbs, and unhealthy food for weeks or months; what is does to the body. You begin to gain weight, feel sluggish and tired, run the risk of high blood pressure, skin breakouts, and undesired moodswings. P.S. men have mood swings too. What do you do to cleanse your body from all of this? You begin to diet and exercise, go on a detox or liquid diet to flush out excess waste, and you replace the bad stuff with the good. Well, the same goes for your spiritual body; to detox you begin to rid yourself of unhealthy connections and relationships, you exercise another level of control and begin to meditate on God's word. You also replace the bad thinking with words of healing, uplift, encouragement, and affirmation. We replace the club life, for group sessions to network and inspire one another, we replace gossip with encouragement and testimony, we replace selfishness with giving our first fruit to God and being a blessing to our communities. We replace gang-banging with Entrepreneurship and Mentor programs for the lil'homies. We replace sexual immorality and adultery with saving ourselves until marriage, and refraining from sleeping with someone out of covenant. We replace degrading and devaluing our children with words of affirmation and attention. We replace job hopping with owning businesses and employing one another. We replace robbing and stealing with hard work and integrity. These are the steps to detoxing, removing harmful substances and unhealthy patterns. As Mark 7:21-23 says "For from within, out of the heart of man, come evil thoughts, sexual immorality, theft, murder, adultery, coveting, wickedness, deceit, sensuality, envy, slander, pride, foolishness. All these evil things come from within, and they defile a person." We have to remove from within and stop looking to blame someone else, or look for the answer outside of self. Everything you need to become a better, healthier you, starts from looking in the mirror and acknowledging who and what you want. Take this time to begin the process and watch the unfolding of God's promises align. Flush it out of your system and being to digest the foods (behaviors) of substance.

Psalm 51:10 (NLT)

"Create in me a clean heart, O God, and renew a right Spirit within me"

1 Corinthians 3:16 (NLT)

"Do you not know that you are God's temple and that God's Spirit dwells in you?"

Proverbs 6:16-19 (NLT)

"There are six things the Lord hates, seven that are an abomination to him: haughty eyes, a lying tongue, and hands that shed innocent blood, a heart that devises wicked plans, feet that make haste to run to evil, a false witness who breathe out lies, and one who sows discord among brothers."

**Self Reflection: What do you have to get rid of, and be honest!

_____
_____
_____
_____
_____
_____
_____
_____
_____
_____
_____
_____
_____
_____
_____
_____

With Thanksgiving

Blessings to My Kings and Queens:

We have so much to be thankful for, our Father in Heaven is so gracious and kind. His mercy endureth forever, and before I send a group text to my contact list, post on social media, wish everyone I meet a beautiful morning; I will first give thanks to the one who made all things possible. I will give thanks for the victories seen and unseen, give thanks for the love and peace we have access to daily, and give thanks for the Life of Christ. Because when there was no one willing to come off His throne and sacrifice His life for me, Jesus did it first. When I needed an example of how to live in the Word and be glad in it, Jesus did it first. And when I needed to be forgiven, transformed, and made new, Jesus washed me first. So I encourage you to give thanks to our King Yahweh, because Jesus did it first! Outside of the material possessions that God has blessed us with, we are more grateful for the children we were/are able to bear, we are grateful for the families and support systems we have, we are grateful for the sound mind and ability to make good decisions. We are grateful for the restful nights we have and not tossing and turning because our Spirit is not at ease, we are grateful for the godly connections and friendships that help us grow, we are grateful for the times our soul was saved from harm or danger, and we are grateful for the lessons we've learned from those experiences. No matter what we've gone through in life, there is never a time we can look back and not see God's hand moving or His power not being lifted. Even when we didn't deserve it, we can feel His love near. But because we are a stiffnecked people, because we are too selfish at times to acknowledge our position in the turmoil, we would rather curse God for a trap we created ourselves. We didn't recognize that though I've sinned, though I've messed up, and I reap the negative consequences for my actions, the Lord still granted me mercy. His grace was still made perfect, and that's why should be full of praise and thanksgiving. Giving thanks for all He has done and celebrate knowing that the pressures of the world couldn't break us.

Repeat this Prayer

Thank you Lord for being the Author and Finisher of My Faith, Thank you Lord for being a good, good father, for loving me so. Lord we honor your name and give gratitude for the power and spirit you've bestowed upon us. Thank you Lord for making us the head and not the tail, for setting us above and not beneath, for calling us worthy in your sight. Lord we praise your wondrous name, El Shaddai, as you've prepared us for the mighty works set ahead of us. Fulfill your will in us, dear Lord, manifest your word through us, and be revealed in my life for the Glory of God to reach the multitude of nations.

In the name of the Son, Yeshua Hamashiach

Lamentations 3:22-23 "Because of the LORD's great love we are not consumed, for his compassions never fail. They are new every morning; great is your faithfulness."

2Corinthians 4:15 "All this is for your benefit, so that the grace that is reaching more and more people may cause thanksgiving to overflow to the glory of God."

Psalm 100:4 "Enter His gates with thanksgiving and his courts with praise; give thanks to him and praise his name."

**Self Reflection: What are you thankful for?

_____

_____

_____

_____

_____

_____

_____

_____

_____

_____

_____

_____

_____

Wasted Energy

Blessings to My Kings and Queens:

Sometimes we just have to say a prayer for renewed strength, to gain our focus and energy back to help us through. Instead of praying for Yah to take this cup of suffering away, similar to what Jesus did in the garden of Gethsemane, we sometimes just need to keep pushing toward the mark (Luke 22:39-44). Right before Yeshua was scheduled to make the ultimate sacrifice and be crucified at the cross, he was filled with angst, but knew to call upon the Lord. Asking the Lord to remove the cup of suffering, the moment of persecution, and the final performance of glorifying the Father by defeating death. Jesus cried out in agony, sweat turned into blood, and was comforted by an angel, because He knew the Father's Will must be done. How many of you, in the midst of trying times, you've overcome battle after battle, and this last one had you asking God to remove it instead of enduring long-suffering. There are times when we are stressed out and tired of fighting, ready to give up and throw in the towel; but angels of Jehovah Shalom grant us all peace and understanding to stand strong. His peace gives us rest in Him, and let us not grow weary as our Spirit is refreshed. It is that moment of comfort we receive, when we stand firm on God's NEVERTHELESS. We won't give up and we won't give in; because our brother in Christ has shown us, that although things may not be what it seems, nevertheless; the Lord's will shall prevail. It is necessary during the tough moments of trial and trouble, that we mount up in His wings and be refueled. Just as Jeremiah 31:25 proclaims, "I will refresh the weary and satisfy the faint." God will refresh us and give us new strength and power to endure. And as you seek that peace, pray that those around you find peace and refuge in the Lord too, because sometimes carrying the burden of someone else can be heavy. Teach them through your relationship with Yah, to cast their cares upon Him. Invite others who are broken in Spirit and dealing with moments of defeat to pray and fast with you, to open themselves up for Yah to search the crevices of their heart. To bind up the wounds of the afflicted, and Heal their troubled hearts. This strategy builds a group of believers who are able to console one another and share in the refuge of the Lord. This strategy breaks the heavy yoke of shared struggle and pain; replacing it with the feather of His wings. These are the habits that help us regain our energy and focus more on the things that give life and restoration, allowing us to replenish everything we had lost.

Jeremiah 31:23-26

This is what the Lord Almighty, the God of Israel, says: "When I bring them back from captivity, the people in the land of Judah and in its towns will once again use these words: 'The Lord bless you, you prosperous city, you sacred mountain.' People will live together in Judah and all its towns—farmers and those who move about with their flocks. I will refresh the weary and satisfy the faint."

In Jesus name Amen

**Self Reflection: What am I allowing to waste my energy, what or who am I attached to that drains me, instead of pouring into me. What am I constantly doing that is not producing?

_____

_____

_____

_____

_____

_____

_____

_____

_____

_____

_____

_____

_____

_____

_____

Signs, Miracles, and Wonders

Blessings to My Kings and Queens:

Some of us can relate to miraculous wonders happening in our lives since the very beginning of our days. We may not always acknowledge those moments, or see them as miracles until time has passed and we are able to reflect on the experiences we have overcome. But they are/were signs of wonder and majesty. For instance, growing up in foster care and having parents that love us, surviving the grimy streets of inner cities across the world, defying the odds and making it out of poverty, overcoming the stigmas of mental illness and disability, being healed of life-threatening diseases, and accidents are all miracles. And while we reference the Holy word for similar situations, we can attest to the goodness of God's glory right in our own homes. With Spiritual eyes and discernment, you too can reflect on the times God has saved you or a loved one, brought you through a difficult season, and answered a prayer of yours. Sometimes as believers, we get too caught up in the miracles performed when Jesus walked the Earth, that we lose sight of the miracles performed yesterday in our own lives. Not to discredit those signs and wonders, but God is a God that was active 4,000 years ago, and is still active now. Knowing the Lord saved a family member from gun violence, a parent overcoming the addiction of drugs or alcohol, seeing a sister beat the perils of prostitution or abusive relationships, a brother surviving the detrimental battles of prison, and losing the hatred we garnered for an absentee parent; are signs of God's faithful hand too. These ARE miracles of a true and Living God, who was, who is, and who's to come. And it's a blessing to know there are greater things He plan on revealing to you. So take a moment and count it all joy, for the testimony you hold, is full of miraculous deeds and saving grace.

Hebrews 2:4 (NLT)
"And God confirmed the message by giving signs and wonders and various miracles and gifts of the Holy Spirit whenever he chose."

I like how the new living translation says "whenever he chose" meaning according to His will, might, and power He can do miraculous things. Whenever he chooses, he can decide to gift you with a breakthrough right in the midst of your pain. When the doctor said no, when the loan didn't go through, when the family tore apart, when the job became tiresome; He chose to gift you a blessing! Because we serve a Father who love us and desire to see His goodness at work for us, we can trust Him and know He'll perform a miracle on our behalf.

Job 5:8-9
"If I were you, I would go to God and present my case to him. He does great things too marvelous to understand. He performs countless miracles."

Lord we thank you for signs, miracles, and wonders!

Self Reflection: What has God confirmed in your life, through His many signs and wonders? Where in your life have you seen a miracle?

_____

_____

_____

_____

_____

_____

_____

_____

_____

_____

_____

_____

_____

_____

Bad Company

Blessings to My Kings and Queens:

As you become more and more entrenched in the word of God and wash yourself from the bad habits, choices and beliefs you once had; you will begin to size up the people around you. You'll ask yourself this question, "Are my friends disrupting my progress, are they spiteful and full of negative energy, do bad things keep happening to my family because of their own treacherous ways?" Sometimes it is necessary to switch up your circle and dissociate yourself from people that will cause you to stumble or question your new beliefs and practices. Everybody does not have your best interest, nor are they looking to grow in the ways of God as you are. Proverbs 22:24-25 says, "Make no friendship with a man given to anger, nor go with a wrathful man, lest you learn his ways and entangle yourself in a snare." You'll find yourself getting caught in the traps of other petty, ill-willed people, going back to what's common. Once you've realized the progress you've made and how the things you used to indulge in, no longer excite you, you'll start having a different outlook on whether or not you can entertain these individuals. 1 Corinthians 15:33 reminds us, "Do not be deceived: Bad company ruins good morals." You can have all the good intentions in the world, but if those around you are wicked, mean, disrespectful, irresponsible, lack good judgment then you'll be easily swayed into moving like they do, responding how they would, or rationalizing sin in the same manner they do. Have you ever met someone who wasn't "bout that life" and they began hanging around people who are, before long, that person is tainted, talking different, and moving like the crooks he/she associate with.

Jay Z said it best, "Once a good girl's gone bad, she's gone forever. I gotta live with the fact I did you wrong forever." Once a person has been changed by life circumstances or the corruption of bad company, it is difficult to come back from that, some people are changed forever. We can all relate to someone who used to be sweet as pie, and now have the attitude of a villain, their hearts are hard, and anger has made them difficult to even talk to. Be careful to not pick up this energy and become like the enemy of this world full of hate, division, and strife. Stay in good company cause birds of feather flock together!

Galatians 1:10
"Am I now trying to win the approval of human beings, or of God? Or am I trying to please people? If I were still trying to please people, I would not be a servant of Christ."

Proverbs 13:20
"Whoever walks with the wise become wise, but the companion of fools will suffer harm."

Psalm 26:4-5
"I do not sit with men who lie, nor do I consort with hypocrites, I hate the assembly of evildoers, and I will not sit with the wicked."

Self Reflection: Father God I pray that you teach me to move away from bad company, Lord replace those who leech and take from me with people who can grow with me and walk in righteousness. I pray that you remove the appetite and desire to be in the midst of bad company, I no longer seek to be full of hate and gossip, nor do I want to reap a bad return because of the company I keep. Teach me to be genuine and respectful of others, teach me to be wise in speech and conduct. May my friendships glorify you, and bring you in remembrance of your word. Oh God, I thank you even now for hearing my voice and moving on my behalf.

In Jesus name, Amen

A Squad Built to Win

Blessings to My Kings and Queens:

One of the greatest things you can do for yourself is gain accountability partners, friends that are not afraid to pray and fast with you, to fellowship and meditate on God's word, to trust the process when things don't appear to make sense. Working together with one another for the purpose of glorifying God, overcoming generational curses, breaking free from addiction and toxic thinking; are all threats of the enemy. Satan does not want to see us working in harmony and getting things done, loving one another and building together. There was even a time in the Book of Genesis, when the Lord saw unity amongst His people and how well we worked together, that He sent confusion down upon us. The Lord said, "If as one people speaking the same language have begun to do this, then nothing they plan to do will be impossible for them" (Genesis 11:6). When we are in agreement, striving toward the same goal, there is nothing that can stop us. There is nothing blocking our ability to support, encourage, uplift, and fight together, as we share a common enemy. And our common enemy is anything that dare to stand against us, as we do not fight against flesh and blood, but principalities. So we have to collaborate our efforts and fight the problem, or injustice, or circumstance that comes up, not the individual or vessel being used to present the conflict. For most people, it is difficult to separate the two, and we end up fighting with the very people, that were sent to us as partners and angels of defense to help us. Mark 3:13, reveals how Jesus went upon a mountain to pray to God and called to him those whom he desired. And he appointed twelve disciples (whom he also named apostles) so that they might be with him and he might send them out to preach, and have authority to cast out demons. He appointed: Simon (to whom he gave the name Peter); James the son of Zebedee and John the brother of James (to whom he gave the name Boanerges, that is, Sons of Thunder); Andrew, and Philip, Bartholomew, Matthew, and Thomas, and James the son of Alphaeus, and Thaddaeus, Simon the Zealot, and Judas Iscariot, who betrayed him. Now looking at the individuals Jesus appointed, some were go-getters, they weren't prim and proper, they weren't perfect and without blemish, but they were faithful and willing. Peter did not play about Jesus, he was ready to defend his friend and go the distance, though he denied Him at times. James and John were brothers, they were close to Jesus and nicknamed Sons of Thunder because of their fiery temper. They brought the storm with them, there was loud rumbling in the air when they came to conquer for God's kingdom. Do you have partners who will bring the thunder, are your friends, supporters, and close associates willing to call down the Heavens and pour out Heaven's resources to get you all to the next level? Can you count on Judas to play his part, are you strong and confident enough to trust God and know that even Judas serves a purpose? When its easy to be in agreement with everyone else and all on the same page, we try to pray away and cast down the very people that God sends to mature us, grow us, rebuild us, or propel us to new heights. Consider your disciples (friends) in the same manner that Jesus did, allowing them to each serve a purpose and fulfill a duty.

Proverbs: 27:17
"Iron sharpens iron, and one man sharpens another."

Genesis 4:9

Then the Lord said to Cain, "Where is Abel your brother?" He said, "I do not know; am I my brother's keeper?"

**Self Reflection: Who's holding you accountable, who's willing to kick a field goal when you don't have the strength to run anymore, so that you all get the victory and Championship!

_____

_____

_____

_____

_____

_____

_____

_____

_____

_____

_____

Hear and Obey

Blessings to My King and Queens:

A warm congrats to my Naomi for stepping out and obeying God's word. The people are ready to receive and respond to the Kingdom call. This daily word is dedicated to you!

Deuteronomy 6:4-9
Hear, O Israel! The LORD is our God, the LORD is one! "You shall love the LORD your God with all your heart and with all your soul and with all your might. These words, which I am commanding you today, shall be on your heart. You shall teach them diligently to your sons and shall talk of them when you sit in your house and when you walk by the way and when you lie down and when you rise up. You shall bind them as a sign on your hand and they shall be as frontals on your forehead. You shall write them on the doorposts of your house and on your gates."

Very specific direction and commandments we were given by Yah, this time more clearly and assuring, the Lord reminds Israel, we are chosen and set apart. And as we come into our Promise land, please obey what has been commanded. Listen and be diligent in our works, share His word and live our lives according to what is written, for His promises are upon us and our children will feed off the inheritance of our faithful labor. We shall experience life more abundantly, gifted and prosperous, peaceful in fellowship, mighty and willful. What has Yah whispered in your heart, what was the message or preview revealed to you, and you have yet to accept? Can you be obedient to hear Yah's word and move when He tells you too, can you build an Ark without there being a storm like Noah, can you take your wife and move your family to an unknown place like Abraham, can you purchase land right before a famine like Jeremiah, can you start the business without having a customer, and can you claim Victory in the marriage that seems like its falling apart? It may not be popular, it may not look possible, you've never seen it done before, but you're willing to obey what was told. And you're willing to share this truth with your children, other believers, and even the lost sheep. This is how we turn things around in our favor, this is how we expand God's Kingdom, and this is how we help others move into the light of the world.

Exodus 19:5
"Now if you obey me fully and keep my covenant, then out of all nations you will be my treasured possession. Although the whole earth is mine"

2 John 1:6
 "And this is love: that we walk in obedience to his commands. As you have heard from the beginning, his command is that you walk in love."

Shalom my sisters and brothers!

Self Reflection: What have you heard from the Lord, and have yet to obey? Do you follow the commandments of the Law, that Jesus Christ fulfilled? Are you obedient in love, are you filled with meekness and humility, do you have self control, and faith in the One who knows all?

_____

_____

_____

_____

_____

_____

_____

_____

_____

_____

_____

_____

_____

_____

Gift and Curse

Blessings to My Kings and Queens:

If most of your time is spent focusing on the areas of brokenness and lack inherited by your family; when will you have time to study the gifts and talents of your loved ones. Though some of them chose to use it for evil, in your hands the curse can be broken. Submit yourself to Yah's will and allow Him to use you for the kingdom: to build, plant, and restore the land for your inheritance. Allow the mistakes of your parents and grandparents to be used as a stepping Stone to get you closer to generational wealth, anointing, and legacy in the name of Jesus Christ. We are no longer a product of our environment but a product of our choices, and we choose to walk in the steps ordained by our Lord and Savior. Yes its true that some of our Fathers were slick-talkin hustlers, they knew supply and demand better than the top CEO's, so lets use those skills for good. We know how to network and bring in clientele, its in our blood, but we won't use it to push illegal candy to the most vulnerable people in our community. Some of our parents were athletic, had speed and stamina that would outrun the top NFL running back, but life happened and they only used this skill to hop the fence and dodge the law. Not us, we're staying the course and getting better at our skills, we're developing ourselves to be better than the circumstances that swallowed our relatives into the belly of the beast. Your mother's love was unmatched, it was unconditional, and though she didn't guard it properly or knew how to lend it in a healthy manner, we are choosing to accept it as a gift. We are creating boundaries and parameters to share this love with others, we are learning to remove ourselves from unhealthy situations, and vipers who prey on our vulnerability. We are using that gossiping Spirit of grandma who sat on the phone all day talking about what happened down the street, and instead spreading the good news of God. Let me tell you about what He has done for me, and willing to do for you too. "Scuse' me, you have a minute, let me share this product with you; buy one and tell your friend to tell a friend." And now here you are building financial stability off of the very things that hindered your loved ones from progressing. Breaking the yoke of bondage and defeat from your neck and getting in alignment with the Shepherd, who lead you to green pasture. Green pasture where you can plant and feed, water and multiply, where you can give access to others and opportunity to the less fortunate. Don't remove the landmark of your ancestors, but instead, remember where they left off, learn from their mistakes and turn yo' lessons into blessings. Shout out to Chance the rapper for that plug, one of the realest verses I ever heard (Song:Best Life ft Cardi B).

Deuteronomy 30:19
"I call heaven and earth to witness against you today, that I have set before you life and death, blessing and curse. Therefore choose life, that you and your offspring may live"

James 3:10
"From the same mouth come blessing and cursing. My brothers, these things ought not to be so."

**Self Reflection: What generational curse has been deeply rooted in your family, that you are now confronted to break? Depression, Poverty, Drugs, Promiscuity, Arrogance, Single parent…Repeat this: Lord thank you for breaking the chains of _____

_____

_____

_____

_____

_____

_____

_____

_____

_____

_____

_____

_____

_____

Put A Praise On It

Blessings to My Kings and Queens:

The book of Psalms speak heavily on thankfulness, gratitude, and praise especially in the midst of a storm. It's full of hymns and moments of worship which is what God delights in. Psalm 28:7 says "The LORD is my strength and my shield; My heart trusts in Him, and I am helped; Therefore my heart exults, And with my song I shall thank Him." During a time as tragic and testing as the pandemic COVID-19, when people are searching for hope, have been impacted by the loss of employment and resources, family members are dying before our eyes; how do we then send praises to the Lord in spite of. Some trials can be a little heavier than others, some battles can draw out more casualties than we would like to admit, and sometimes Yahweh requires our attention in full surrender of Him. This time in particular came upon the Earth without warning, it has paused the movement of everyone, and interrupted the activities of everyday life. With all of the shelter in place stipulations, the social distancing, and the need to quarantine; we have been forced into isolation with the True and Living God. A Father who loves us so much that He has chastened us, called us out of the darkness and into light. Every nation, every idol, every tongue, and knee is bowed to the Almighty Elohim. We praise Him on high, we thank Him for renewing our strength and granting us new mercies every day. We exalt His name for being El Shaddai, we glorify his majesty, and we find refuge in the bosom of His wings. No one loves us like He does, no one gives us comfort like the Lord, no one brings us joy in the morning but the Mighty God we serve. With arms stretched wide, and eyes gazing toward the Heavens, we all send praises up in unity, together. Regardless of color, creed, status, age, or preference; Jesus Christ is Lord; and we have been saved by the blood of the Lamb. I want to remind you to keep a song of praise on your lips and thank the Lord for all that He has done and watch your victory come to pass! We overcame this difficult time and saw the salvation of the Lord, because we believed, because we humbled ourselves and gave Him our praises, because we asked for forgiveness and repented of our sins, because He gave His only begotten son, we Won.

Isaiah 25:1
"Lord, you are my God; I will exalt you and praise your name, for in perfect faithfulness you have done wonderful things, things planned long ago."

Revelation 5:13
"Then I heard every creature in heaven and on earth and under the earth and on the sea, and all that is in them, saying: "To him who sits on the throne and to the Lamb be praise and honor and glory and power, for ever and ever!"

**Self Reflection: What did this time remind you of, and how were you able to praise your way through?

(1x1x1=1) One Accord

Blessings to My Kings and Queens:

Let God prevail you in purpose before connecting you with partnership. Sometimes it's best that God order your steps and direct you in the position of your calling before mating you with a spouse; because it gives you more time to become disciplined, faithful, and focused on your goals. Instead of trying to balance your time to maintain a relationship and forcing something to work with someone that you are not equally yoked, we can be diligent about our passions and dreams. One of the worst things we can do is force an unhealthy situation, or realize that you've married someone in your not yet season. And now you guys have outgrown one another, grew to despise each other, or deal with challenges in every area of your marriage with tests not assigned to you. What if you spent more time focused on the things that bring you joy, getting to know yourself on levels unimagined, and learning a new skill or trade. What if you became one with the Lord and discovered all the things you needed to heal from, do inventory and assess what your flaws and insecurities are, or spent time evolving and awakening new desires. See the journey of finding your purpose is different from just stumbling upon life experiences; because sometimes things we experience without preparation causes setbacks, we don't enjoy them as much or understand why they had to happen. How many of you can relate to enjoying life more when you explore your options and go at things head on, you're seeking these moments to happen; as opposed to wandering the earth without vision and direction and coming across something you weren't prepared for? The great preparation becomes a season of isolation, intention, and reconciliation. The old habits and lifestyle choices we made during our wilderness season, the time we got caught up in the world, serving our flesh, is being transformed into evolution, growth, and acceptance. Similar to King David, we realize how teachings and experiences of our past help mold and shape us into who we would become in our Promiseland. David knew that he could slay Goliath, because he had spent much of his youth slaying lions and bears. It was the same strategy, the very lessons he learned preseason, would help him accomplish his purpose and calling later in life. It is at this point when we've accomplished and past those tests, spend time making better decisions, and understand what we want out of life; that Yah begin to connect us with Kingdom partners. He'll arrange moments to happen, or give clarity to authentic relationships that are Heaven sent. Marriages that are heaven sent, are ordained and joined by Yah, a set of events will transpire, that bring two in agreement for the fulfillment of His plan. Genesis 2:24 says, "Therefore a man shall leave his father and his mother and hold fast to his wife, and they shall become one flesh." Two becomes one flesh after He (man) has tended to his garden and began the work of the Lord just as Adom did, just as Abraham did, just as Isaac did. Ruth was tending to the garden and working the land when Boaz found her, Queen Esther was chosen out of the Beauty pageant, Rachel was hidden until Issac worked seven years in the field to gain her love. Be found doing God's work, and walking in purpose before He connects you to your Purpose partner (husband/wife).

Ecclesiastes 4:9-12

"Two are better than one, because they have a good return for their labor: If either of them falls down, one can help the other up. But pity anyone who falls and has no one to help them up. Also, if two lie down together, they will keep warm. But how can one keep warm alone? Though one may be overpowered, two can defend themselves. A cord of three strands is not quickly broken."

**Self Reflection: What is your Purpose?

_____

_____

_____

_____

_____

_____

_____

_____

_____

_____

Daily Declaration

Blessings to My Kings and Queens:

One of the main points we have to consider when we begin to evolve is reprogramming ourselves, speaking things as though they are, and re-establishing who we are. Because the world will remind you of who you used to be, old friends won't understand the new you, and even your own thoughts will condemn your progress; we must daily decree a new identity. In Ephesians 4:29, Paul spoke about Spiritual strength, "Let no corrupting talk come out of your mouths, but only such as is good for building up, as fits the occasion, that it may give grace to those who hear." When you've experienced difficulty or a life of trial and tribulation, hearing the naysayers come against you, and everyone who claimed "you wouldn't be nothin" it becomes difficult to quiet the noise and get back on track. Everyday we have to look in the mirror and speak words of affirmation to ourselves, our children, and our loved ones. Remind yourself that, "I am great, I am powerful, I am worthy, I am strong, I am forgiven, I am blessed, and I am healed." Building up self confidence, dispelling the myths of what others say, and being bold about it, allows us to release the insecurities of shame, guilt, and that less than mentality. We get to reframe the picture we see and perspective we have, we get to color in the lines of what we want our future to look like, and we also get to redefine our today by walking away from the past. I remember growing up as a little girl and being told how beautiful I was, my grandmother would tell me when I came home from school, "hey sweet girl what did you learn today? Did you dare to raise your hand and stand out?" My grandmother was affirming positive words and attributes over me, that helped to shape my identity. It gave me a level of confidence to be different, to be a trendsetter, I didn't have to fit in or fall into peer pressure. She was asking me if I raised my hand, if I was bold enough to answer questions and not be afraid of looking stupid, or was I just sitting in the background hiding my gifts. Growing up in a close knit family, had its perks, it taught us to have a sense of pride and unity. The family dynamic prepared us for the real world, we were already familiar with the culture vultures, we knew who to be on the look out for, we knew who to watch from a distance, because society was coming to break you down. Like Biggie said, " To all the teachers that told me I'd never amount to nothin' To all the people that lived above the buildings that I was hustlin' in front of…Called the police on me when I was just tryin' to make some money to feed my daughter (it's all good)." There were people that didn't want to see you win, and there were people too small minded to believe you can and have changed. Teachers spoke negative about you, parents who said you're just like your father, systems of oppression that tried to make you a villain because of the color of your skin, unhealthy arguments that tried to tear you apart; its cool, cause You are greater than those lies. Since you don't live for them, you're not caught up in the "he say, she say" theatrics of gossip, and you know you're self worth; then it becomes easier, to stand firm on what God says about you. And once you have become confident in who you are and what is written about you, it lend toward your ability to support and inspire others. A self-assured person is humble enough to help someone else shine without dimming their own light. The same grace extended to us in the process of maturity, we can extend to someone else and not let corruption, double-mindedness, or negative thoughts hinder us.

Declare a new thing over your life, accept the decrees of royal citizenship, adoption into a Kingdom family with Christ. Speak it, Believe it, Achieve it!

Matthew 5:14
 "You are the light of the world. A town built on a hill cannot be hidden."

**Self Reflection: What have others said about you that is not true? Record your voice speaking positive affirmations and listen to it daily... Your Spirit will begin to attract and become more of who you declare yourself to be!

_____
_____
_____
_____
_____
_____
_____
_____
_____

Small Skill, Large Impact

Blessings to My Kings and Queens:

Some of us never live within our own capacity, and sometimes minimize our impact in the world due to comparison. Truth is, we spend so much time comparing our gifts and talents to others on a larger scale, that we forget how great we are in being our true authentic selves. For example, King David knew he couldn't fit into Saul's armor, so instead he went to defeat Goliath with the armor he was most familiar. Ready to slay a giant with 5 small stones and a sling shot; he didn't need a hi-tech weapon or army, and just like David had all he needed, so do you. Gideon knew the Lord of Hosts that his ancestors spoke of, but he also needed to experience God for himself, so he prayed that God reveal himself before battle. His ability to get confirmation from God and walk in the commandments of the Lord, granted him favor in battle, and allowed for him to have a larger impact than expected. He didn't need 300,000 to win the war, but his faith in the Lord and 30,000 soldiers was enough to see the Power and Greatness of God manifest. These are examples of small deeds that eventually had large impact on the movement of a people, and created opportunities of change. God is a God who rewards obedience, He doesn't look for ways to bless you the same way someone else has been blessed, He doesn't repeat His goodness, but God is wanting to perform new miracles. You were created for a time as this and your inventions, creations, and skills are needed. Be so engulfed in your abilities and perfecting your skills, that you won't have time to look to the right or left of you and compare. Stop trying to fit into someone else's shoes and become so comfortable and skilled in your own, that even giants fall, just like David. You are enough! Amazon is a large company that gathers and house the resources of small businesses and everyday people, like you and I. Mom and Pop shops have had more consistent success than franchise restaurants because customers are looking for that original, authentic service. Working in a small local community or school gives the opportunity to encourage and uplift hundreds and thousands of children who will eventually become productive adults; these positions are viewed more honorable and worthy in the eyes of God than being a CEO or top exec. Our ability to change the world, happens one deed at a time, one move at a time, one idea at a time, and it takes people like You and I to be all that we can be. Find your niche, that thing you do well without extreme effort, and do it with all you got. It'll be well received and very much needed, because there is a lane carved out just for you.

1 Samuel 17:38-40
says Saul said to David, "Go, and the Lord be with you." Then Saul dressed David in his own tunic. He put a coat of armor on him and a bronze helmet on his head. 39 David fastened on his sword over the tunic and tried walking around, because he was not used to them. "I cannot go in these," he said to Saul, "because I am not used to them." So he took them off.

** Self Reflection: Why have you compared yourself to others and refuse to accept your uniqueness? What makes you great, what makes you stand out?

_____

_____

_____

_____

_____

_____

_____

_____

_____

_____

_____

_____

_____

_____

_____

Great Investments

Blessings to My Kings and Queens:

A wise woman is considered an investment. She is worth far more than rubies and gold. In Proverbs 3:15 it reads" She is more precious than jewels, and nothing you desire can compare with her.Long life is in her right hand; in her left hand are riches and honor.Her ways are ways of pleasantness, and all her paths are peace.She is a tree of life to those who lay hold of her; those who hold her fast are called blessed." Now the history of this text is believed to come from King Solomon, one of the greatest and wealthiest men of Yah, who reigned for 40 years. A wise man who valued wisdom, moral integrity, and divine direction from the Most High. Proverbs 3:15 compares wisdom to a woman, because the power of a woman can inspire and uplift her husband to be who God called him to be. She is more precious than jewels, because the beauty and gentleness of a godly woman is deemed valuable and pure. Long life is in the hands of wisdom; the ability to make sound judgment and apply discernment to life choices based on past experience and knowledge, gifts us with longevity. A strong, confident, woman who fears the Lord, is like a tree of life, she bear good fruit and others can eat from her garden. She shares intellect and healing, she walks in modesty and power, she is full of patience and kindness. Just like wisdom is a gift that pours into you daily, so is a Queen sent from God. Connecting to the wife of your youth and a woman of profound purpose is a great investment. Her children calls her blessed, and those who know her, respect her dearly. She honors her marriage and her husband is favored, he walks in the boldness of his anointing and lead with confidence. And

when trouble tries to creep in and disrupt their union, they stand on the promises of God and the vows they made to one another. They tackle the problem and not the person, they recognize the importance of accountability and forgiveness, and they grow stronger together. Let your marriage, friendships, and connections be filled with pleasantness and peace. Full of life and power, for blessed are those who invest in the kingdom of God, seeking His righteousness daily.
This is the Wisdom of Solomon, that should also be found in Husband and Wife.

Proverbs 15:22
"Without counsel plans fail, but with many advisers they succeed."

Genesis 24:64
"So she became his wife, and he loved her."

Ecclesiastes 4:9
"Two are better than one, because they have a good return for their labor"

**Self Reflection: What have you invested in and have not seen a good return? It may be time to re-assess the relationship and make sure it is centered on the wisdom of God.

_____

_____

_____

_____

_____

_____

_____

_____

_____

_____

_____

_____

_____

_____

Work, Werk, Wurk

Blessings to My Kings and Queens:

Work. Work. Work. Work. Work….in my Rihanna voice, that is what it's gonna take to repair the broken communities, dysfunctional families, and confused lifestyles of my sisters and brothers across the world.
Alot of us can speak on the conditions of the world and discuss the severity of danger, lack of resources, and detriment of mental health. But until YOU step in position and accept the assignment God gave YOU, then things will not change. We've heard the agendas of those who believe its someone else's job to come in and save us, we've heard the agendas of the privileged communities who expect us to pull ourselves up by the bootstraps and fight without weaponry, and we've even heard the agenda of those in denial about the history of certain ethnic groups. But truth is, now is the time to accept the charge of Elohim and walk in the Sovereignty of His will. Nothing is going to change until we as a people stand in unity, acknowledge where we have fallen short, and begin to build up a nation who walk with integrity, love and care for one another, respect the G-Code, and establish constructive companies for the betterment of mankind. We've experienced enough of the world's temporary relief and gratification in self-serving agendas, violating one another, robbing and stealing from one another, degrading our women, disrespecting our men, abusing our children, and selfishly honoring other Gods. Share your gifts and talents to bring forth goodwill, learn the art of forgiveness and forbearance, tap into the fullness of who you are and allow others to glean from your abundance. Don't just help others when it's convenient for you, but help

those in need because it is our duty. John 9:4 says "I must work the works of Him who sent Me while it is day; the night is coming when no one can work." Meaning we were sent here to break strongholds, fill the gaps of parenthood for orphans, educate one another in love and discipline, build wealth and opportunity and so much more. Get in line if you're tired of things being out of bounds. And stop looking for Blankman, Damon Wayans character to come and be a reject superhero. The work that has to be done requires us, me and you to be on the frontline. Creating the opportunities, educating our children, caring for our homeless, rebuking the wicked, calling on our men, and storing up treasure for those to come. Celebrating our Heavenly Father and acknowledging Him in all of our ways, instead of idolizing the celebrities of our time and boasting in ourselves as if we made things happen without Him.

2 Timothy 4:1-9
"I charge thee therefore before God, and the Lord Jesus Christ, who shall judge the righteous and the dead at his appearing and Kingdom; Preach the word, in season and out of season; reprove, rebuke, exhort with all long suffering and doctrine. For the time will come when they will not endure sound doctrine; but after their own lusts shall they heap to themselves teachers, having itching ears; And they shall turn away their ears from truth and shall be turned unto fables. But watch thou in all things, endure afflictions, do the work of an evangelist, make full proof of thy ministry.For I am now ready to be offered, and the time of my departure is at hand. I have fought a good fight, I have finished my course, I have kept the faith: Henceforth there is laid up for me a crown of righteousness, which the Lord shall give me, and not only to me but all of them that love Him. "

2 Chronicles 7:14
"If my people, which are called by my name, shall humble themselves, and pray, and seek my face, and turn from their wicked ways; then I will hear from Heaven, and forgive their sin, and heal their land."

**Self Reflection: Today is the day to make the decision, are you gonna accept the charge?

_____

_____

_____

_____

_____

_____

_____

_____

_____

_____

_____

Let Go and Let God

Blessings to My Kings & Queens

One of the greatest things we can do is hand our worries and cares over to the Lord. He wants us to be so dependent on Him that our life is not our own, but is used for His Glory and all the experiences in it will be a testimony of Victory. In a wilderness season, we are tested by some of life's toughest battles that causes us to harbor these feelings of hurt, anger, bitterness, and fear. We go through things that force our hand, some things that knock us down, and test our Faith. I can remember having a conversation with a friend one day, and they were like, "Man…I went through some tough situations and hard times, but it wasn't until I hit rock bottom that I realized I really needed God." And I began to help them understand another way to look at it, maybe God never left you and He was always in the background looking out for you. But what if, you had to be exhausted of all options, left with nothing and no one but you and Him. God knew as long as you had a plan b or plan c, you would "swindle your own way out" but if He knew that rock bottom will bring you to Him, by any means necessary, He'll get your attention. And that's how it is with most of us, we hold on to the things we don't want God to work on, or we feel, Lord take this and I'll handle the other stuff. Trying to separate our dysfunction, and God is telling us, give me all of your cares, all of your heart, all of your insecurities, all of the things that cause you to be double-minded; and I'll heal it. The Lord want to extend His peace, joy, understanding, and mercy; so that you'll be able to withstand and move forward into the Promises He has made. Just as He did in Exodus 13:21, "And the Lord went before them by day in a pillar of a cloud, to lead them the way; and by night in a pillar of fire, to give them light; to go by day and night:He took not away the pillar of the cloud by day, nor the pillar of fire by night, from before the people." This is when God led the children of Israel out of Egypt and out of captivity, with no other option, they had to trust that He would make a way. They had to trust in His direction and His provision, even if it came through the cloud of smoke or pillar of fire. Letting go of things that hold you bound, frees up space, time, and energy inside of you to do more productive things, and focus on greater. Not by your own might will you see a way out, but by His Spirit you too will overcome, just as our forefathers have done. Let Go of the control, the need to be right all the time, the perfectionist Spirit that prevent you from moving even though you don't have it all together. Let Go of the unhealthy relationships you're attached to, let go of the bitterness you've been storing up in your heart because people have done you wrong. Let go of the insecurities you've held on to that helps you pacify your situation and never take ownership. Let go of the excuses you've made as to why "IT" never happened for you. And let go of the need to blame others, when you're receiving everything you've fallen for; people treat you the way you've allowed them.

Hebrews 12:1
"Therefore since we are surrounded by so great a cloud of witnesses who by faith have testified the truth, stripping off every unnecessary sin which so easily entangles us, let us run with perseverance the race that is set before us, looking away from that will distract us, focusing on Jesus, the Author and Finisher of our Faith."

Proverbs 3:5-6

"Trust in the Lord with all your heart and lean not on your own understanding; in all your ways acknowledge Him, and He will make your paths straight."

**Self-Reflection: What are you holding on to that you have yet to give over to God?

_____

_____

_____

_____

_____

_____

_____

_____

_____

_____

A Shepherd's Voice

Blessings to My Kings & Queens

God will use whomever He chooses and some of us have overcome situations and experiences simply for the purpose of relating to others. We have to lend compassion and grace by the power we know and re-present God's people to Him without fear of connection. So don't assume you are the only one who has felt discouraged, unworthy, counted out, or confused. Because all of the things you've experienced, were meant to place you at the feet of His throne, share your wisdom, and speak your truth for the Freedom of nonbelievers. You are the reason they can confess the mighty power of our Lord and Saviour, your testimony will be used for the kingdom to break every chain and set every captive free. And now they too can Believe in the Creator of the Heavens and Earth. Vengeance is His and Victory is Yours! John 10:27-30 declares, "My sheep hear my voice, and I know them, and they follow me. I give them eternal life, and they will never perish, and no one will snatch them out of my hand. My Father, who has given them to me, is greater than all, and no one is able to snatch them out of the Father's hand. I and the Father are one." So as a Shepherd, Yeshua is speaking in this moment to explain what it looks like to be a leader, to gather men and women and lead them to the True and Living God. It is a task that should not be taken lightly, and it is important to try our hardest to live a life of reproof and discipline that will not lead others astray. When you think of it from the perspective of a caretaker, someone who has been entrusted to care for someone else's child and love them like their own; make sure they are fed, they are protected, and they are taught good moral. These are the same attributes, the Lord is requesting we have, to care for God's children, to feed them His word, protect them and look out for one another, and also make sure our actions align with integrity and morale. That is not an easy task, and if you have grown up in the church or have experience with Baptist, Pentecostal, COGIC, teachings then you are also familiar with church hurt. As with other denominations, there were teachings and doctrine that was being fed to the Sheep (congregation) that did not always coincide with the lifestyle of those teaching it, nor did it coincide with biblical principles. Not all but some, had more traditions, waywardness, and people "playing church" on Sunday than they were walking the walk. It became an Us vs Them mentality of saints and sinners, who on the surface looked the same. Other than the Bible in the car, the church gossip, and the Sunday visits; there wasn't much of a difference in how sinners lived and those that were so called "saved." They were still cursing up a storm, having sex out of wedlock, honoring pagan holidays, only crying out to God when they needed something, abusing their spouses, committing idolatry, and coveting over the blessings of someone else. This is what it means to lead someone astray, to present this image and front like they were living this way, but behind closed doors, that was not the case. And Jesus is telling us, this is what we are moving away from. I am sending Shepherds out to the field with wolves and serpents, who have taken advantage of my sheep, (my people) and it is time that we deliver them from the hand of the Enemy. Be prepared to go through spiritual warfare, be prepared to chase after those that wander off, be prepared to extend compassion and meet them right there are. Your sheep will know your voice, and they will recognize that you were sent by the Most High, because I and the Father, are one.

Isaiah 53:6
"All of us, like sheep, have strayed away. We have left God's paths to follow our own. Yet the Lord laid on him, the sins of us all."

Jeremiah 23:1
"Woe to the shepherds (pastors) who are destroying and scattering the Sheep of my pasture!" Declares the Lord.

**Self Reflection: What have you been called to Lead?

_____

_____

_____

_____

_____

_____

_____

_____

_____

Jesus….You Rang?

Blessings to My Kings & Queens

Why is that some of us so easily hit the ignore button, snooze button, or leave a message on read when it comes to God? It is time to wake up, and move on the promises of His word. Ain't nobody "sleepin on you" but you. You were made for so much more and we have gotten so comfortable with doing the bare minimum, pleasing self, and minding our own business; instead of doing what we are called to do. Well the latter is what allow others to take advantage of our sons and daughters, getting in situations where "we don't care about other people and what they have going on." And in turn others don't care about us and what happens to us. I can remember growing up in a neighborhood that was more like a community, everyone knew each other, looked out for each other, and were not afraid to tell kids to stop doing something that they knew the parent wouldn't approve. Times have changed and we care less about what the next person is dealing with, we have become selfish in withholding information that will help someone else grow, and we have refused to respond when Yah calls us if it means, inconveniencing yourself for the greater good. When it comes to our own dreams and agenda, we'll set the appointment, be there on time, and check anyone that did not play their position. But when it comes to answer the call of purpose or serving others, we hit the snooze button, we refuse to answer, or hit the ignore button, like oh that's not my problem. Can you imagine if Yah thought this way about us, if He was so selfish and inconsiderate when we needed Him, that He ignored our cry, or ignored our worship. Where would be if He left our prayers "on read" where would we be if He denied the appointment to heal us or save us out of a situation. Well that is how God sees us in moments like this, that He sent us to be angels on earth, servants and co-workers of His to look out for each other, and help one another in the time of need. Young men and women who have been abused need us, those in prison and have been casted off need us, children being molested and neglected need us, the elderly need us, and the we have to get in position to care, spread light and goodness, and also be of service.

Isaiah 66:4 says, "So I will choose their punishments and will bring on them what they dread. Because I called, but no one answered; I spoke, but they did not listen and they did evil in My sight and chose that in which I did not delight." Until we answer and respond accordingly, life is gonna keep destroying our families, our schools, our health, our finances, our government, and our beliefs. Step up in the name of the Father, Son, and Holy Spirit, because we are needed and the call has been made.

John 15:16
"You did not choose me, but I chose you and appointed you so that you might go and bear fruit-fruit that last- and so that whatever you ask in my name, the Father will give you.

1 Peter 2:21
"To this you were called, because Christ suffered for you, leaving you an example, that you should follow in his steps."

**Self Reflection: Whose call have you ignored, what part of the community, have you denied?

_____
_____
_____
_____
_____
_____
_____
_____
_____
_____
_____
_____
_____
_____
_____

Faith Over Fear

Blessings to My Kings & Queens

It's soooooo hard learning to overcome fear, and we sometimes make it even harder with our own thoughts and beliefs; pre-setting our doubts on a situation. There are circumstances that happen in our life that causes us to fear, or be afraid of things going right, because they have gone wrong for so long. Instead if we learn to reprogram our insecurities to focus on the task at hand and what Yah expects us to learn from it, it will move us closer to where we ought to be. Joshua 1:9 says "Have I not commanded you? Be strong and courageous. Do not be afraid; do not be discouraged, for the Lord your God will be with you wherever you go." God is with us wherever we go and His plan is to prosper and not harm us, so we must learn to trust the process and have bold Faith. This scripture happens when God is commanding Joshua to move forward and prepare to take over the land He has promised us through our ancestors. Joshua is leading the charge to overtake land and power in more than three battles ahead, and ill equipped, he is pondering whether or not God will be with him. Faith that is anchored on the belief that He has done it once, and will do it again, help us to move boldly in the face adversity, and just like Joshua we can trust that "He will be with us wherever we go." Faith that you know things will get better and you'll overcome yet another trial, another bad relationship, another failed opportunity, another lost job, another doctor's report, another failed test. The objective is to ignite faith over fear, and conquer the very thing that scares you in the moment. This can be done overtime, one task at a time, building up your courage, trusting God's hand when it is moving, and declaring over that mountain that dare to stand in your way. Be confident in the word and study scripture that helps direct you in the way you should go. Because sometimes the very things we fear, are the things we were never supposed to be apart of, or that which God places before you in order to gain your trust. He wants us to trust Him, and rely on Him with every part of our being. Your faith is made strong during those spiritual battles that test you and require you to believe what you have yet to take hold of. I like to define Faith with the concept of a movie trailer, going to the movie theater and seeing a trailer or 4 minute snippet of the next film coming to theaters soon. There is a release date, an expected or appointed time that God will bring this movie, this reality to fruition. And He gives you a preview, or highlight of that dream, that vision that will become reality at the appointed time, just as He promised. And though we don't know when, how, or see that our current situation does not align with what we're expecting; we can bank on that preview, that confirmation He gives us, to know it will come to pass.

Hebrews 11:1
 "Faith is the assurance of things hoped for, the conviction of things not seen."

Romans 10:17
"So faith comes from hearing, and hearing through the Word of Christ."

2 Corinthians 5:7
"For we walk by faith, not by sight."

**Self Reflection: Where lies your Faith?

Armed for Battle

Blessings to My Kings & Queens

I can remember one of the first verses we had to memorize in Summer Bible camp growing up was Ephesians 6:11-18. "Put on the full armor of God, so that you can take your stand against the devil's schemes. For our struggle is not against flesh and blood, but against the rulers, against the authorities, against the powers of this dark world and against the spiritual forces of evil in the heavenly realms. Therefore put on the full armor of God, so that when the day of evil comes, you may be able to stand your ground, and after you have done everything, to stand. Stand firm then, with the belt of truth buckled around your waist, with the breastplate of righteousness in place, and with your feet fitted with the readiness that comes from the gospel of peace. In addition to all this, take up the shield of faith, with which you can extinguish all the flaming arrows of the evil one. Take the helmet of salvation and the sword of the Spirit, which is the word of God. And pray in the Spirit on all occasions with all kinds of prayers and requests. With this in mind, be alert and always keep on praying for all the Lord's people."

And while I was too young to understand why, I now get the jist of it. It's TRUE, we don't fight against flesh and blood but the powers of this dark world. So we must be armed and ready for battle, surrounding ourselves in truth, standing strong in the Spirit of God as our words season the earth, walk in peace, and keep our thoughts in obedience to Christ so that we are not bound to the pains and trauma of attack. Because none of us are exempt from the tests and trials that God has pre-ordained in order to help elevate us, refine us, and mature us in the way we should go. I can remember a time that people would say, "oh you must be going through that because you ain't saved, or yeah they keep living like unsaved heathens, and that's what happens." Not realizing that the tests and battles we face in this life are not always tricks and schemes of the Enemy, take it from someone who does believe in the Most High and try my best to walk upright in the statutes and commandments of Yah's word. Just because I am "saved" or has been baptized and cleaned from my sins, does not mean that life's adversities are not gonna test me. Though my battles are not as tough or life threatening as nonbelievers or sinners, does not mean I won't have to go through a pressing and positioning. Even in the Kingdom, God is looking to elevate us from glory to glory to glory, so while no my feet will not stumble, and He will clear my path, there are lessons I must learn in order to do what ever assignment God has placed before my path. And there also times when the Lord is pointing out the division of flesh and spirit that we will continue to battle and fight. We will overcome the world if we maintain our posture and not let our guard down to the enemies schemes. Regardless of the season change, from spring, summer, fall and winter; make sure your inner garment protects you from the ways of the world; we can always switch up the outerwear.

Hebrews 4:12 "For the word of Yah is living and active and sharper than any two-edged sword, and piercing as far as the division of soul and spirit, of both joints and marrow, and able to judge the intentions of the heart."

Isaiah 59:17 "He put on righteousness like a breastplate, and a helmet of salvation on His head, and he put on garments of vengeance for clothing. And wrapped Himself with zeal as a mantle."

**Self Reflection: In the morning, when you rise out of bed and thank God for waking you up, be sure to put on your greatest armor, dress to impress…Helmet of Salvation, Breastplate of Righteousness, Belt of Truth, Shoes of Peace, Sword of the Spirit, Shield of Faith, and Prayer. With this attire, you can cast down the fire. The fire that tries to attack your mind, body, and Spirit. Teach this to your children, it'll be a great weapon of salvation.

Butler Season

Blessings to My Kings & Queens

So one of the things Yah has done for me in gifting me with Spiritual eyes, is that I now see situations more clearly. I understand what it means to be of service, and how He places us in different positions to magnify His kingdom. His righteousness does not just reign in the church or tabernacle, but also in our homes, workplace, and everywhere else He sends us. Learning to use your gifts and talents for the Glory of Yahweh, will have you preaching, teaching, singing, uplifting, and feeding His sheep in every part of the world; just as John the Baptist did before the coming of the Lord. Not many of us get excited about helping others, being a team player, or servant that stands in position to elevating the platform of others. Why is that, why do we have the mentality that if it's not about me then, No, I don't want to be apart. Or we look at situations for what we can get out the deal, and be compensated for our services. Well the truth is, we are to be help to one another that we so desperately pray to God about, when we ask the Lord to send provision, or send the right opportunities, or send the help we need; He doesn't send an alien or foreign object to answer the prayer and provide what we were missing. Answered prayers come in the form of You and I; whether that's financially, spiritually, emotionally, or physically. We are sometimes called to be ushers, butlers like Jeffrey from Fresh Prince, and help move along the agenda of God's will. Are you humble enough to accept the role of helping your sister manifest her dreams, are you willing to put in work and help your brother excel, are you willing to bless someone in paying the bills, or are you willing to pray and declare healing over someone fighting a health issue? Because truth is, that is a selfless act, it requires a humble Spirit of someone who is not self-serving or looking to Glorify themselves, but more so someone who is confident and self-assured. When you know who you are, and that helping someone else shine does not dim your light or blow your candle of purpose; you are then willing to encourage, inspire, and support others. Just like John the Baptist, who knew from the beginning, his calling was to usher in the coming of the Lord, it was to prepare hearts and fix everyone's mind on Jesus Christ. He was sent to turn us from our wicked, evil, worldly ways and repent for our transgressions in order to walk in a holy, blessed way. John the Baptist taught us the word of God, the fullness of God, and the purpose of the Son, who was his blood cousin. Can you imagine being the forerunner to your cousin, and being sent to prepare the stage for them without feeling insecure or jealous. John went around town, professing the truth, and risking his life, baptizing people in water; before the time had come for Jesus to walk in his calling and prepare for the cross, also baptizing in fire. That's no easy feat, and not many of us can honestly do it, we have a problem with sharing the spotlight; but in the book of John we see this done with zeal and gratitude.

Luke 1:15-17 says
"He must never drink wine or strong drink, and he will be filled with the Holy Spirit, even before his birth. He will turn many of the people of Israel to the Lord their God. And he will go as forerunner before the Lord in the spirit and power of Elijah, to turn the hearts of the fathers back to their children and the disobedient to the wisdom of the just, to make ready for the Lord a people prepared for him"

John 1:25
" They asked him, then why are you baptizing, if you are neither the Christ, nor Elijah, nor the prophet?"

Matthew 11:11
" Truly I say to you, among those born of women there has risen no one greater than John. Yet the one who is least in the kingdom of heaven is greater than He."

**Self Reflection: Who have you been called to assist, and be a butler?

_____

_____

_____

_____

_____

_____

_____

_____

_____

_____

_____

Mixed Messages

Blessings to My Kings & Queens

You know some sinners (nonbelievers) justify their behavior by saying "God knows my heart" when they're doin wrong. How many of us can relate to that term, as we have found it so fitting when things are convenient for us to indulge. Well isn't that why 2 Timothy 2:15 tells us to Study to show thyself approved unto God, a workman that need not to be ashamed, rightly dividing the word of truth. Paul is reminding Timothy as a leader in Christ; in this life it's not enough for God to just "know our heart" but we must study and show ourselves approved and pleasing in His sight. Regardless of the distractions around us, let our yes be yes and our no be no. Dividing the truth in times of opposition and times of triumph; not being ashamed to stand firmly on what we say and what we do, for this reveals our true heart and character. It's almost like the dysfunction of a relationship, when someone is telling you one thing but their actions are showing something totally different. How can you say you love me but are willing to disrespect me or violate my trust; love does not keep score, it does not take prisoner to hold hostage. Have you ever been in a situation when you told someone the things they did hurt you, and they vowed to never do it again, but a couple months later you all were back dealing with the same type of problem? Like really, how could you still do the very thing I brought to your attention and told you, hurts me or causes me pain. That is a form of abuse, a deliberate attack or action to hurt me over and over again with knowledge of what you are doing. Well this is how God sees it, when He says "These people come near to me with their mouth and honor me with their lips, but their hearts are far from me (Isaiah 29:13)." We walk around saying we love God, we honor and worship Him, but yet we do things that hurt Him and cause affliction to others. If God knows your heart, let it be written in the Book of Life that you chose to live a life that edifies Him, that exalts Him, and Glorify Him because of all the great things He has done for you and the trying times He has seen you through. Not just for the Lord to know your Heart, but see that your actions align with someone who prayed Psalm 51:10, "Lord create in me a clean heart and renew a right Spirit within me."

May Yahweh bless your next relationship/marriage to be filled with integrity and honor, may the two of you walk in harmony and not be ashamed to align your unity with sound doctrine just as Christ came to do. May others see Yah's love be manifested, nurtured, and cultivated through you.

Amen

Self Reflection: What mixed messages are you sending, what are you on the fence about?

_____

_____

_____

_____

_____

_____

_____

_____

_____

_____

_____

_____

_____

_____

Prized Possessions

Blessings to My Kings & Queens

Can you relate to the feeling of getting something you really wanted and learning to be responsible, protective, and careful. Like there was a time, we would be so excited to get a new toy, a new bag, or outfit, or even a new gadget from someone who thought enough about us. We would be so guarded about that time, unwilling to share or break it, we would put it up when company came over, or we would keep it in our book bags hidden from plain sight. Where did we go wrong, how did we lose the sentiment of taking care of ourselves and others the way we would our most prized possession. Why do we value cars, clothes, and jewelry more than we value life, love, and the pursuit of happiness? Luke 12:34 says "For where your treasure is, there your heart will be also." Oh man, just sitting here writing this devotional, I'm thinking of a time I got something that I really valued and saw as treasure. I literally kept it in my jewelry box, and even when I didn't wear it, I would check on it daily. Going back and forth to the jewelry box to open it and make sure it was right where I left it, as if it would walk away or disappear. But truth of the matter is, how did we lose that, how do we no longer see a reason to check on one another, to tenderly care for the hearts of our sisters and brothers? Or even ourselves, allowing pain and affliction to set up shop in our bodies, along with toxic behaviors and attitudes, selfish ambitions and scheming agendas. Some of us are looking for a way out by simply preying on the weak, or scamming and swindling others out of what they have earned. Card cracking, identity theft, robbing, stealing, conniving, attention seeking, social media plots, negative feeding through music and media; we indulge in it all. Let's learn to treasure and honor self again; as God's most prized possessions, let's consider how valuable we are, that He saw fit to sacrifice His only son for You and I. Let's see each other as the apple of God's eye, the elect, you are beautiful, you are handsome, you are smart, and you are worthy. God goes to His treasure chest, just like I used to do with my jewelry box, and breathe life into you, checking to see if you're ready to turn from those old ways and finally accept Him as your Lord and Saviour. He's checking to see if you are still exactly where He left you, or have you wandered off again, trying to do things your way, following the ways of your own selfishness; or have you surrendered, are you found in the Garden like Adom and Eve.

Deuteronomy 26:18
" And the Lord has declared this day that you are His people, treasured possession as He promised, and that you are to keep his commands."

Isaiah 43:4
 "Because you are precious in my eyes, and honored, and I love you, I give men in return for you, people in exchange for your life."

Exodus 19:5
 "Now therefore, if you will indeed obey my voice and keep my covenant, you shall be my treasured possession among all people, for all the earth is mine."

Self Reflection: How good is to know we have such a Good Father, who sees us as prized treasure. A love so true, that He is willing to exchange anyone for your life, giving other people in return for you.

Save Some for Later

Blessings to My Kings & Queens

Soooo...I was talking to someone the other day and they were like ooh I gotta taste for some hot wings from one restaurant, an Italian ice slushie and cheese fries from another restaurant, and they went to get it, just like that. Well it made me think how impulsive we are as a people, without hesitation or second thought, we get ourselves in these situations without thinking about the consequences because we only know to feed our wants and desires. Just like this scenario, my friend wanted a little bit of this and a little bit of that, regardless if it required an inconvenience drive from one place to the next. When it comes to our appetite, we'll do whatever makes us happy in the moment, whatever delivers that instant gratification, a quick fix. Maybe if we save some for later, simply learning to restrain ourselves and become disciplined in our habits, we'll have better judgment, make wiser choices, and have healthier outcomes. What if we made better choices based on what is available, based on what God has already provided, and not look to take a number 7 from here and a number 4 from somewhere else. Then we can better gage what it is we truly desire from God, especially since He knows what we need and not just our wants. Not in the sense of you're settling by eating at one location, but you're making better use of the menu and really trying to see if they have everything you can begin to appreciate. Or you're learning to scale back and sacrifice the quick go-to for a more healthier, satisfying option. Just like in relationships, instead of fooling around with this person and that person, simply because you can't laugh with this one, or this one is too whatever. Save some for later, and refrain from indulging in those right now moments, because God is preparing you for someone who'll come along and meet most of your expectations without you ever needing to ask them. A gift from the Most High, suitable just for you that doesn't require you to pick and choose from more than one person, or seek contentment elsewhere.

1 Corinthians 3:16
Do you not know that you are God's temple and that God's Spirit dwells in you? If anyone destroys God's temple, God will destroy him. For God's temple is holy, and you are that temple.

Galatians 5:19-21
Now the works of the flesh are evident: sexual immorality, impurity, sensuality, idolatry, sorcery, enmity, strife, jealousy, fits of anger, rivalries, dissensions, divisions, envy, drunkenness, orgies, and things like these. I warn you, as I warned you before, that those who do such things will not inherit the kingdom of God.

**Self Reflection: What fleshly desires have you been feeding that require you to scale back, sacrifice, or completely do away with?

_____

_____

_____

_____

_____

_____

_____

_____

_____

_____

_____

_____

_____

Friend Vs. Foe

Blessings to My Kings & Queens

Understand that the enemy cannot forcefully use someone who doesn't have the ability to shift or change the trajectory of your life in the same way he can use a Friend, a loved one, someone you trust. But please remember it is still a purpose they serve, a lesson for you to learn, or become a stepping stone to elevate you higher. Let them set your table and watch you Eat. It is normally the people within our inner circles, those that are closest to us; that will cross us, hurt us, and take advantage of us. I can remember so many times in the past how growing up and watching the news about family members who stabbed, murdered, or set someone up to get hurt. And I would think like, Lord why would someone do that, what would cause a friend or relative to do such a thing. And it wasn't until I faced something similar, that I realized the magnitude of hate, jealousy, and selfish motive of other people. The Spirit of jealousy is real, the Spirit of trauma is real, and it will consume a person to the extent that they provoke harm onto others. I was so hurt and offended to see someone that I trusted, that I held in high regard, willing to cross me and use me for selfish gain. But I also learned through prayer and understanding that Yah will use our adversary, whether friend or stranger to set our table, to be a footstool, and catapult us in the direction that the Most High ordained. Not many people around you have the ability to hurt you, we don't really take it to heart when someone we don't know offends us; but the hand of our brother in battle will break us, causing us to not trust others again. Learning to forgive these individuals and free yourself from the bondage of their brokenness, gives you freedom. It sets you free to guard your heart and be conscious of the company you keep, it reminds you to set boundaries with others, and always trust that Yah will use people to teach you the principles of life, even if it means trial and tribulation. Luke 22:2 says, "and the chief priests and the teachers of the law were looking for some way to get rid of Jesus, for they were afraid of the people. Then Satan entered Judas, called Iscariot, one of the Twelve disciples. And Judas went to the chief priests and the officers of the temple guard and discussed with them how he might betray Jesus. They were delighted and agreed to give him money. He consented, and watched for an opportunity to hand Jesus over to them when no crowd was present." This scenario in the Bible shows us how one of the chosen men appointed by Jesus, our beloved Emmanuel, was sent to complete prophecy. Judas was assigned to be the one who betrayed Jesus and send Him to the cross, after Satan had entered him. And here it is, just like our Saviour, we too get surprised and caught off guard when people we love and care about are consumed with the Spirit of Satan and betrays us. But rest assured, it is not the person but the evil intentions and malicious behavior that causes them to act that way, and we have to rebuke those ideas, thoughts, and attitudes down. We have to silence and cut off the plans of the enemy who dare come against us and our bodies; whether that is an uncle or family friend who molested you, a spouse or mate who abused you, a parent who left you or called you unworthy, a cousin or sibling who betrayed your trust, or anyone else who took advantage of you.

I speak healing in that area of your life and cast down every demonic force or plan that dare try to kill your purpose and dream. And if the deed is assigned by Yah and placed on the calendar for a time as this, I speak to your strength and endurance that you persevere in the midst of adversity. A friend or foe, regardless of how we see them, they are sent to fulfill the Will of the Lord.

Amen

Exodus 23:22 "But if you will carefully obey Him and do everything I say, then I will be an enemy to your enemies and a foe to your foe."

Psalm 44:10 "You make us retreat from the foe, and those who hate us have taken plunder for themselves."

Train of Thought

Blessings to My Kings & Queens

Learning to take hold of your thoughts and behavior is a lot easier than we give ourselves credit for. I was talking to a friend one day, and right in the midst of the conversation, he was like oh man wait..I lost my train of thought. And as I began to ponder on that concept and what it means to lose a train of thought, lose the very idea or thought you had, that it literally escapes you. In that moment my friend was caught in the middle of his story, sharing something with me, and then out of nowhere it was gone. Well it made me think of scripture, 2 Corinthians 10:5 says "We demolish arguments and every pretension that sets itself up against the knowledge of God, and we take captive every thought to make it obedient to Christ." How often do we forget to practice this very concept and demolish arguments that set itself up against the knowledge of God. We don't have to entertain frivolous conversations, or sit around and have unproductive debates about who's the best this, who's flyer than who, or why do you think that happened that way. Instead we can take captive every thought or belief in our mind and bring into obedience to Christ, literally thumbing through our mind as the conductor of our train. Controlling what we think and what we decide to daydream upon, our plans and strategies, our execution of walking in purpose, all of it should be submitted unto God. And that will then help us cast down what doesn't belong, what thoughts have come to their last stop and must depart, and also what memories are still taking up space where new ideas should live. Every day it is a task to control the train of thought and ideas we have, and make sure when in conflict with someone else, we don't let our reaction or be driven by hate, selfishness, insecurity, or anger. Because people will do things and say things to provoke you but learning to demolish argument and division under the authority of God shows true power and self control. Being the conductor of your train and not allowing productive thought or concepts escape you, and instead holding onto the principles of life that allow you to stand in remembrance of God's word. Recall what is written about you, meditate on it, and remember to do what it is you've been chosen to do. Anything that dares stands against that, must be demolished.

Ephesians 6:17 "Sword of the Spirit"

You have the sword of the Spirit which is the word of God, in order to demolish the arguments and gossip of people who don't believe in you, people who doubt the move of God, and systems that are designed to trap you in.

Isaiah 55:8

"For my thoughts are not your thoughts, neither are your ways my ways," declares the Lord.

Self Reflection: What thoughts have you had, that you must purge and get rid of, how can you better filter through what you think and believe?

_____

_____

_____

_____

_____

_____

_____

_____

_____

_____

D.O.A. (Dead on Arrival)

Blessings to Kings & Queens

One day I was driving somewhere, which I do a lot. Laugh out Loud! But I was on the highway, passing old corn fields, open land, herds of animals, you know the kind of stuff you would normally see when taking a road trip or driving down South. Well this particular trip, I happen to see a lot of road kill on the side of the road, dead carcasses and animals left on the shoulders of the highway. And it made me think, D.O.A., Dead On Arrival. That is what a person is labeled when the EMT team arrives to a crime scene and the body cannot be revived, they are termed, D.O.A. Well it made me think what is it in our lives that have to die off before we walk into this next season, before we arrive and rejoice in the Promise land, there is some baggage we have to release and toss aside. We're gonna have to break some chains off; chains of lies, perversion, identity and confusion, generational turmoil. The poor behaviors of smoking and drinking, sitting around in idleness, wasting time away, speaking the Lord's name in vain, putting oaths on His head with blanket statements like "On God" The disillusion of our lustful desires, doing what we want without precaution to other people, selling our souls for attention, and manipulating people to hustle them out of something for personal gain must die away before we arrive. Having sex before marriage, forgetting to make our children a priority, being halfway dedicated to the works of our hand must die away before we arrive. We are killing those things that no longer serve us, and focusing our energy, time, and abilities to Grow and Mature in the goodness of what is Ahead.

Ephesians 4:22 reads "to put off your old self, which belongs to your former manner of life and is corrupt through deceitful desires, and to be renewed in the spirit of your minds, and to put on the new self, created after the likeness of God in true righteousness and holiness." God requires us to put away our old self and walk into a new creation, in the likeness of Christ himself, free from sin and disbelief. Free from our old ways of thinking and selfish desires, and dress up in the armor of peace and salvation. Don't just bury those things but kill them off so that they don't resurface in our times of frustration and fear, so they don't resurface in the lives of our children's children or our space of comfort. Bad yokes that have a stronghold on us, damaged relationships and deceitful thoughts that cloud our judgement, do away with those things and be renewed by the Holy Spirit.

Psalm 32:8 "I will instruct you and teach you in the way you should go; I will counsel you with my loving eye on you."

Romans 12:2 "Do not conform to the pattern of this world, but be transformed by the renewing of your mind. Then you will be able to test and approve what God's will is-his good, pleasing and perfect will."

2Corinthians 5:17 "Therefore, if anyone is in Christ, the new creation has come: The old has gone, the new is here!"

**Self Reflection: What in your life has to be D.O.A?

What's Your Why

Blessings to My Kings & Queens

Sometimes in the face of adversity it is difficult to stay the course and remain on the right track, but when your Why is far greater than the circumstances you're facing, you'll endure all things with determination and heart. Never forget your core values, regardless of what you've experienced, regardless of what has been thrown at you, and who's standing in your way. Life happens to all of us, and we can get so down on ourselves, that we forget why we even started the job, why we decided to get married, why we became parents, why we joined that industry, or why we started the business. It was the pursuit of a dream, it was to change the lives of those around you, it was to make a better life for yourself and family, it was to experience the goodness of what Yah promised us. Remember your why, and hold on to it, place it in front of you and keep running toward it, because someone else is counting on you, children being abused need your childcare facility, or expertise as a teacher, the police union need you to step up and take the position to help change the stigma, Congress needs you to run for office and fight policies that affect us, the health field needs your innovative ideas for treatment, and the world needs to hear your story of Triumph. Now this is not to discredit those already making contributions or currently succeeding in the Entertainment industry, but we need more films to represent our community and tell our stories, we need music that uplift our young women and encourage our men, we need more business owners and less employees to build generational wealth. It is you that we need, and Yah created you for that very purpose. Take the time to recoup from setbacks and refocus so that you are not easily distracted or taken off course. Ignite the Spirit of courage and boldness to walk in confidence, and stand firm on what you believe. In Romans 5:3 the word says, "And not only this, but we also exult in our tribulations, knowing that tribulation brings about perseverance; reminding us that tribulation builds perseverance, the perseverance to see a thing through to completion." Continue to persevere to see those ideas come to fruition, to see those vision boards come to life, and to see the manifestation of Yah's will on Earth as it is in Heaven.

Don't stop, don't give up, don't turn back, and don't beat yourself up for the troubles you had to endure. Taraji P. Henson didn't get her big break until her 30's, Ava Duvernay just learned filmmaking a few years ago, Toni Morrison (rest in paradise) wrote her first novel at 39, Samuel L Jackson was 43 years old in Jungle Fever, Puff Daddy reinvented himself 4 times, and will still come with a switch up to rebrand himself. Young Jeezy took the street hustle and grind to Corporate Thuggin, knockin' down glass ceilings left and right. Let no one tell you what you can and cannot do, Remember your Why and Shatter Everything in the Way.

**Self Reflection: Prayer

I pray that everyone reading this is filled with hope and perseverance that no matter what they are faced with, they know that Yah's purpose and will is to bring those promises to pass. His love for you is greater than the Love we have for ourselves, and I pray that you always feel and experience the Hand of Yah in your life. May your life be a monument of glory and riches and honor of the Most High, a testament to all things working together for the good of those who Love the Lord. Nothing and no one can prevent His will from being done in your life, so stay focused, and see the salvation of the Lord. Be steadfast in your works, be intentional about your walk, and accept the lessons along the way. Because although it may not be easy, it will be Worth it.

In the name of Yeshua….AMEN

You Mad or Nah?

Blessings to My Kings & Queens

How many of you can relate to the jedi mind tricks of relationships. You know like when a woman is upset about something and the man is just supposed to know what's wrong, or when a man expects all these things to be done when he gets home, as if you haven't been working all day too. We've had the conversation before so I shouldn't have to tell you why I'm mad, "you should already know" mentality is not only dangerous, but extremely dysfunctional too. In relationships we play the games of assumption and comparison all the time, and that's what causes friction and disagreement. Some of us carry the baggage of a previous relationship and expect our current partner to mimic some of that same behavior, if so and so was a liar, when my new guy says this, that means he's lying too. Or if my last girl was scheming and conniving, then when my new girl does something similar, unknowingly, that mean she's scheming too. When we don't address the problem or communicate in a healthy fashion with one another, things begin to fester. And the more that things fester, we begin to look for ways to one up each other, making the other person "feel it" seeking revenge or preparing for attack. I know you're tired of talking about it, but until the problem is solved or the situation changes, we may have to keep bringing it up. And it's not to nag or get on one another nerves, but it's simply to clear the air. If we get complete understanding the first time, it won't be necessary to discuss again, but what happens when the offense is made again. Do we keep explaining ourselves to someone who knowingly causes us pain or refuse to hear us when we're communicating. The bible says, "let's not quarrel or be in constant strife, it causes division amongst the house." We don't speak the same language as our mate does and the different situations that affect us, may not be an issue for someone else. So at times, it may take different techniques and strategies for them to know our love language, stay in the Word of God and study your mate.

Proverbs 21:19
It is better to live in a desert land than with a quarrelsome and fretful woman.

Proverbs 17:14
The beginning of strife is like letting out water, so quit before the quarrel breaks out.

Proverbs 15:18
A hot-tempered man stirs up strife, but he who is slow to anger quiets contention.

Self Reflection: Learn to Express L.U.V.

Listen, Understand, Validate

_____
_____
_____
_____
_____
_____
_____
_____
_____
_____
_____
_____
_____
_____

Way too Soon

Blessings to My Kings & Queens

Have you ever been in a situation and you knew you were being tested, you knew it was a challenge for you. Like based on the things that were happening in the moment, you recognized Yah's hand orchestrating things to happen to you and for you. And unlike the times before that, you waited. You remained calm, steadfast, and in your prayer closet seeking Yah's presence. Because all of us are familiar with premature birth and the complications that come along when something has not fully developed. Don't move in haste because when you put your hand on it, Yah remove His, and that's when things require special attention, care, and sometimes follow ups back to the physician. I know we don't like being patient and want things when we want them, but the Lord said wait until the appointed time, let things come to fruition, and see the Light of His glory bring it to pass. This is no easy feat, especially when its news we want to share, ideas we want to reveal, and opportunities that have come about. We want to share our accomplishments or the moves we're making with people we love, for support and encouragement. But sometimes speaking on something way to soon, can send the Spirit of jealousy on a rampage, it can signal the Spirit of disruption to steal, kill, and destroy your vision. 1 Corinthians 4:5 says "Therefore judge nothing before the appointed time; wait until the Lord comes. He will bring to light what is hidden in darkness and will expose the motives of the heart. At that time each will receive their praise from God." The purpose of this devotion is to help you acknowledge when you have not learned the power of discernment and knowing when and who you should share certain ideas. The threat of premature birth is real and some of us are vicariously moving through life without the confirmation of God's will. And then when things don't work out, we look to blame everyone else who didn't do this or didn't do that; instead of accepting the part we played. I've come to truly admire the time I spend with God and how far I've come on setting every concern, thought, and dream before Him to gain insight and clarity as to what I should be doing to manifest those blessings. When we are used to doing things our way and making it happen, getting the funding, brainstorming the ideas, finding the location, getting the trademark, making the connections, etc; we forget the favor and agreement that God bestows upon us. In our own capacity, we want to show others how hard we worked, how we made it all possible, without acknowledging it was the light of Jesus Christ that accelerated the plans, the light of Jesus Christ that established our success.

In due time all things will be revealed, be still until the Due Date!

Isaiah 49:1

"Listen to me, O coastlands, and give attention, you peoples from afar. The Lord called me from the womb, from the body of my mother he named my name."

**Self Reflection: Be slow to speak and quick to listen, Learn to keep things private during the birthing season and wait until Yah bring it to pass

The Truth Sets You Free

Blessings to My Kings & Queens

There is something about carrying on a lie that does more damage than good. And most times it doesn't serve any purpose but to perpetuate evil, because after its told darkness begin. The dark habits of bitterness, anger, resentment, hurt, fear; just like the myths of our childhood that traumatized us as adults. Once the lie is told, you got to keep it going until some older aged hater tells you the truth in class, "nope Santa's not real ya mom bought that stuff, and oh your tooth goes in the trash after she put a buck under the pillow" The bible reminds us that Jesus answered, "I am the way and the truth and the life. No one comes to the Father except through me." (John 14:6) Dear children, let us not love with words or speech but with actions and in truth. (1 John 3:18)

While the above myths are small and harmless, it sets precedent on how we choose to hide the truth from people when we think its protecting them, we don't wanna hurt feelings, we learn these unhealthy concepts of evil. And the life of Christ is proof that Truth is not about feelings, it's about honor, respect, and light. It is the way to freedom in the Spirit, it casts out darkness, and hold us accountable to being better individuals. I can recall a time I was in a relationship with someone who was extremely insecure, and thought I was always up to something or trying to date someone better than him. It would get to the point where I was explaining myself and proving my innocence for things I wasn't doing. And eventually, it lead me to start telling little white lies to keep the peace, to prevent arguments and disagreement. Until I realized what I was doing, and how convicted I was in my spirit, I began to feel so bad about doing something that didn't represent who I was. I wasn't a liar, and becoming good at it for all the wrong reasons, I knew this wasn't for me. I would rather leave than to be filled with lies and deceit, it's a vicious cycle that's hard to break. It binds you up in darkness and become harmful discourse. So I had to make the decision to walk away, and sometimes that's hard to do, but choose your peace, your sanity, and the truth over everything. That is where your Freedom lie, and in that Freedom, your love for Christ Jesus and His abounding mercy, will teach you to walk in truth and share that with someone worthy.

Psalm 15:2-3 "The one whose walk is blameless, who does what is righteous, who speaks the truth from their heart; whose tongue utters no slander, who does no wrong to a neighbor, and casts no slur on others."

1 John 1:6 "If we claim to have fellowship with him and yet walk in the darkness, we lie and do not live out the truth."

**Self Reflection: Heavenly Father guide us in your truth and teach us for you are God, our hope is in you all day long. We ask that you keep our tongue from evil and our lips from telling lies oh Lord, you are Faithful in all that you do and we need you to transform our thoughts and cause us to speak in truth and righteousness. Be present in our lives oh God, gives us confidence in what is right and may we be pleased with doing well in your sight.

In Jesus name we pray Amen

Children Follow our Lead

Blessings to My Kings & Queens

I can remember growing up and hearing so many people say "oooh, you sound like yo mama. Or girl you act just like your mom." People that I didn't know would stop me and ask, "You Stack daughter ain't you?" That was my father's nickname, He was known around town as "Stack." Here I was, a double dose of my parents, I had the beauty and heart of my mom and a go-getter Spirit like my dad. My fragrance, my aura, my light exuded that of my parents who did a great job I must say. But this is the concept of Proverbs 22:6 Train up a child in the way he should go: and when he is old, he will not depart from it. Not to say that in my youth I didn't make mistakes and get trapped into foolish things as most kids do, but as I got older (wise and ready) I remembered the Word of my Father and teachings of my mother, that I will not depart. Though I strayed, got caught up in sin, got caught in the streets doing what I wanted to do, I knew my way back to the Word that was taught to me, prayed over me, and inscribed on my heart. This scripture has more to do with the leadership and guidance of our parents, and their responsibility to raise us in truth and discipline, as opposed to the poor choices of the child. God gives us free will, and He knows we'll be tempted by the world but after the deed is done, how do you turn things around and walk in reverence to him and honor the parents that equipped you with the teachings of scripture. Our children are truly a reflection of us, sometimes I get so upset when I hear people call their children "bad." Children are not bad, they are busy, they are curious, they are bombarded with threatening spirits to take them off course and cause them to give up their birthright before knowing their true potential. We have to teach our kids constructive ways to have fun, we have to teach them healthy boundaries and work ethic, we have to exemplify real love and compassion for each other. So when others ask, how did you raise such honorable young men, and poised young women, you'll say, "You simply imitate the word of God (Torah), and build on the legacy of your forefathers. Don't be me, be greater than me." Teach this to your children, lay it on their hearts, and show them daily; because there will be a time when you are not around and someone will ask based off their behavior, you such and such child?

Psalm 127:3-4 "Children are a heritage from the Lord, offspring a reward from Him. Like arrows in the hands of a warrior are children born in one's youth. Blessed is the man whose quiver is full of them."

Matthew 21:16 ""Hosanna to the Son of David," they chanted. "Do you hear what these children are saying?" They asked him. "Yes," replied Jesus, "have you never read, "From the lips of children and infants you, Lord, have called forth your praise?"

Deuteronomy 6:7 "Impress them on your children. Talk about them when you sit at home and when you walk along the road, when you lie down and when you get up."

**Self Reflection: What habits as a child have you picked up, and may need to change with your own children?

_____

_____

_____

_____

_____

_____

_____

_____

_____

_____

_____

_____

_____

_____

_____

_____

Yah's (God) Favor

Blessings to My King & Queens

So I have come to realize that the favor of God cannot be mistaken for our good deeds, or something we've earned by working hard. It is instead the unmerited grace and opportunity bestowed upon us because God sees fit to bless us, protect us, and provide for us, for His glory. No one can boast about the goodness of God and make it their own success, i.e. (self-made) because just like He did with Joseph, Noah, Moses, Esther, and so many other bible characters, His hand was evident in their elevation. Joseph had favor in prison and in the land of captivity, Noah and his family was favored out of the entire nation and sent to build a boat before the storms even came. Moses was favored to bring a nation of out bondage, lead them to the Promise land, and have a relationship with God like no one had ever known. Esther was a favored Queen who released her people from the hand of Haman, who planned a massacre to kill them. They were all saved and the plot was then turned on him instead. I pray that your next season is prosperous, full of joy and peace, and abundant in the riches of Heaven, so much so, it send those around you to God's kingdom as they too search for the one who provides. Unless your glow-up is a direct connection to Yah, and forces unbelievers to seek Him, then it is not His Favor but polished distractions from the enemy. Get ready for unexplainable, jaw dropping, unshakable, streams of Favor!

Ephesians 1:11 "In him we have obtained an inheritance, having been predestined according to the purpose of him who works all things according to the counsel of his will"

Proverbs 3:1-4

My son, do not forget my teaching, but let your heart keep my commandments, for length of days and years of life and peace they will add to you. Let not steadfast love and faithfulness forsake you; bind them around your neck; write them on the tablet of your heart. So you will find favor and good success in the sight of God and man.

> ** Self Reflection: Where in your Life have you seen God's Favor?

_____

_____

_____

_____

_____

_____

_____

Don't need more Friends, You need partners

Blessings to My Kings & Queens

When you're working and building something, sometimes the people closest to you won't always invest, give time to support, or help you build; its usually the disciples you meet along the way that put forth the extra energy. It wasn't Jesus' mother or brothers that helped propel his ministry, but the faithful men and women he met along the way, willing to drop everything and join the charge and commission of God's will. We don't need more friends, or acquaintances to network or sit around and share ideas with; but instead we need more partners to hold us accountable, lift us up when times get tough, and support the movement of God's wondrous hand. We need to be surrounded with people that are successful, working towards their dreams, and can help lead us in the right direction. Our circle should be filled with go-getters, hardworking men and women who are not afraid to step out on faith and do whatever it is they were called to do. We need prayer warriors to come in agreement with us and bless the works of our Hand, we need practical people who would buy our product or service and support, we need people that believe in righteous marriages, and believe in building healthy families. We need a team of Johns and James (the Thunderous twins) who will spit fire to the haters and naysayers, we need our own Peter who will cut somebody for you and not let others speak ill when you're not around. We need our own Mary Magdalene who will lend a helping hand and go back to that dream we thought was dead, and let us know "It has risen" get up and get to it, your purpose will not die here. We need a financial advisor like Matthew, making sure the budget is right and you get your fair share, managing and budgeting the coin down to the penny. We need a few partners like the ones Tabitha had, who were not willing to let her go, she meant too much to the community, she had too much to offer, her influence and impact could not die, so they spoke healing and requested Peter anoint her to Rise again. We need disciples who get excited to see demons fall, to see strongholds fall off of your family, to see your children get well, to see your business prosper, to see your community grow, to speak restoration in your life. Start working, build the brand, start the book, create the lane, go back to school, apply for the position, make the move, and those connected to your purpose will attract like magnets. They'll drop their nets and support the vision just as Yah ordered.

Matthew 4:18 says, "As Jesus was walking beside the Sea of Galilee, he saw two brothers, Simon called Peter and his brother Andrew." They were casting a net into the lake, for they were fishermen. "Come, follow me,"Jesus said, "and I will send you out to fish for people." At once they left their nets and followed him.

Hebrews 10:24-25 "And let us consider how to stir up one another to love and good works, not neglecting to meet together, as is the habit of some, but encouraging one another, and all the more as you see the Day drawing near."

Genesis 4:9 "Then the Lord said to Cain, "Where is Abel your brother?" He said, "I do not know; ami I my brother's keeper?"

**Self Reflection: Review your Dream,
Now build your Team**

_____

_____

_____

_____

_____

_____

_____

_____

_____

_____

_____

_____

_____

_____

When Bad days Get the Best of Us

Blessings to My Kings & Queens

Everyone is familiar with the Story of Job, one of the most popular tales of a successful servant of Yah, who was tempted by the devil with permission. The story of Job in the bible is usually referenced to point out how a person who loses everything, regains it all after showing his faithfulness. But as you read further, in this bible verse, consider the conversation Job had with Elihu. Elihu was a young man wise beyond his years, who reminded Job that though you seem to be good in your eyes and don't understand the affliction that has come upon you; Only God can judge, condemn, and correct us. See during the time that Yah allowed the enemy to tempt Job, cause disease to come upon him, completely destroy his livestock, and burn his properties with his children inside; Job was trying to justify and rationalize with God saying, have I not been faithful, curse the day I was born if you find fault in my life. And he was speaking to all of the things he had done for God, lived righteous, remained humble, and devoted his time; when Elihu stepped in to say "Hey can you consider what God has done. El Elyon (Sovereign and Supreme God) one of the many names of God, has dominion over all the Earth and can even allow famine and evil to take place if it means shining light on His glory. His word is law, and His plans are greater than ours, so there will be times when justice is prevailed through trial and performance, not because of our own personal choices, but because it is written. When a person is going thru hard times, it may not be because of their sin or past wrongdoing, it may simply be to teach us to reverence God who made all things possible. He can give us all the glory and riches, or take them away as He sees fit. And still give it back two-fold in our repentance and gratitude. This very thought is not the most favored in the life of a believer, because so many of us have been taught that if we do right, honor God, we will not experience hardship. But we forget Jesus' last words were "I have told you these things, so that in me you may have peace. In this world you will have trouble. But take heart! For I have overcome the world (John 16:33). So we were warned, and Job should have known, to not account for every good deed or work he has done; because God already knows, He is familiar with the works of your hand, and you will be rewarded for it. But you will also have trouble in the earth, you will also have to experience the fire to come out refined, you will be placed in the mouth of a lion so that others can see the Might of your King, and the enemy will have permission by God to test your faith. Be grateful for every season and know that it is part of the grand plan, it serves a greater purpose than we can imagine, and His righteous hand will not let you fall.

Job 40:1-10

And the Lord said to Job:
"Shall a fault finder contend with the Almighty?
   He who argues with God, let him answer it."
Then Job answered the Lord and said: "Behold, I am of small account; what shall I answer you? I lay my hand on my mouth. I have spoken once, and I will not answer;
   twice, but I will proceed no further." Then the Lord answered Job out of the whirlwind and said:
"Dress for action like a man; I will question you, and you make it known to me.

Will you even put me in the wrong? Will you condemn me that you may be in the right?
Have you an arm like God, and can you thunder with a voice like his? "Adorn yourself with majesty and dignity; clothe yourself with glory and splendor.

**Self Reflection: Where in your life have you been tested?

_____

_____

_____

_____

_____

_____

_____

_____

_____

_____

Empty Vessels

Blessings to My Kings & Queens

A lot of people talk about overflow but it's usually for personal gain. But in order for God to replenish your overflow, it has to be poured into others. There has to be an anointing, a transaction, or a deed that occurs when you are sharing, giving, or pouring into the cup of someone else; in order for God to fill you up again. If you're only receiving an outpour and never give unto others, then you will never lose nor gain what it is God has blessed you with. Think about it like this, if I never open a bottle of water, nothing gets in and nothing gets out, so it will sit at the top of the rim, never flowing over. We never know what we're full of until it comes out, so consider this, "what area in your life is proof of your overflow?" Marriage, work, children, ministry, friendships, school, community involvement, helping those in need....they should all be touched by the milk (oil) you spill.

There is this saying I used to hear growing up, "Don't cry over spilled milk" and now I better understand what that means. Don't cry over something that spilled, because it can be cleaned, it can be replenished, and its also proof of overflow. It's proof that you've not only reached the top, but you have more than enough that its now spilling over onto others. 2 Kings 4:4 says; Elisha said, "Go around and get jars from all your neighbors. Get empty jars, many of them. Then go in and shut the door behind you and your sons. Pour the oil into all these jars, and set aside each one that is full." So she went from him and shut the door behind her and her sons. They took the jars to her, and she poured. When the jars were full, she said to her son, "Bring me another jar." And he said to her, "There is not one jar left." Then the oil stopped flowing. She came and told the man of God.

Vessels….the potter and the clay. When you think of clay being molded, the creator (potter) decides what he's gonna make. The clay doesn't then say, "Why have you made me this way?" But it is used for the purpose and intent that the potter created it. Think about it, the clay, the vessel could be formed into a bowl. And depending on the heart of the owner, whether righteous or unrighteousness, good or evil, the owner will use that bowl for eating food or for ashes when smoking. Filling the bowl with cigarettes or blunt roaches, the clay is now being used for the intent and purpose of holding the poison or toxic residue of its owner. Or it can be a bowl for feeding, to hold the food that nourishes the body and lifts the Spirit, for the purpose of sustaining the residue of its owner. In this life we get to choose, as a living vessel, now that the Father has created and molded us, what will be the intent and purpose of our being. What will your body, your temple represent? Depending on the maturity of your heart and the willingness of your surrender, will you let the Lord, the Creator use you for what He had in mind. To represent that which is good, to shed light in dark places, to stand firm on truth, to move in goodness and mercy, to sustain the body of Christ. Or will you carry out the will of the Enemy, the purpose of holding and regurgitating that which is evil, that which magnifies darkness and poison. You're the vessel, the power belongs to you, you have already taken shape and form, for it was pre-destined before you took your first breath, but the choice is yours. See in 2 Kings, when the woman made the decision to obey and retrieve the jars to fill up, she didn't know her outpouring would cause an overflow, that she will be blessed with more... and the more that she gave, she received. She didn't expect a supernatural overflow that would cause excess. But God does exceedingly and abundantly more than we could ask. And here it is, she had enough to pay off debt, and live off for the rest of her life. You don't have to give money, or fancy items, but God is telling us to share what we do have, share your gift, share your time, share your resources; it will be given back, pressed down, shaken together, and overflowing.

**Self Reflection: What fills your Cup?

_____

_____

_____

_____

_____

_____

_____

_____

_____

Build a Bridge, Not a Fence

Blessings to My Kings & Queens

So many times we don't seek Godly wisdom in our relationships and friendships allowing them to just be. Like we'll meet someone and begin conversations or relations with them, never knowing why we ever had the first encounter. Truth is, the reason most situations go astray is because we don't move with intent or purpose. We normally get involved and start title thumping after the first couple dates, or first few interactions; like "you my bae, you gone be wifey, hey bestfriend, what's up bro, hey sis?" In all of your relationships, whether social or professional, Ask God, "who is this person to me and who am I to be to them?" "How can I bring them closer to you Lord and where should I place boundary?" See a bridge can serve one of two purposes, it can separate two parts of a city or neighborhood, and it can also be a merger of the two, bringing them together. And in life, we can consider our friendships and relationships in that same manner, are we to be a bridge that separate a person from the life they used to live and help them move away from the things they used to do, or are we to be a merger, standing in the gap to get them closer to who they are becoming, to help them see the future. We have to learn to be intentional about our connections with others, not everyone is suppose to be a sex partner, not everyone is supposed to be lifetime partners; some are sent for a season, some are sent to help you mature, some are sent to teach a lesson, and some are sent to build with you. Seek wise counsel and understand when God is placing someone in your path, or when the enemy is distracting you on your journey. Be careful not to cause someone else to stumble and fall because we have misunderstood the reason and season, be careful to not treat a stranger with disrespect because you never know when you're entertaining an angel sent to help you. Can you be the one that God looks for, count on, and stand in the gap of your brothers and sisters path? Have you gotten too involved in a relationship trying to be someone's saving grace, and God only called you to help them grow? Have you outworn your welcome on a relationship, you were only sent to befriend and experience childhood with? Have you supported some of your friends and they've helped you accomplish some of your goals, or are you all still doing the same things you were when you all first met?

Romans 14:13 says "Therefore, let us not criticize one another. Instead decide never to put a stumbling block or pitfall in your brother's way."

Ezekiel 22:30 says "I searched for a man among them who would build up the wall and stand in the gap before Me for the land, so that I would not destroy it."

**Self Reflection: Assess your relationships and Ask God to lead you in how you should interact, respond, or serve

You Reap what You Sow

Blessings to My Kings & Queens

Why do we sometimes get mad with God when we begin to reap the bad for things we've done to others. Or why are we so surprised by the return on investment for poor choices and decisions we've made. For example, I've been hearing a lot lately about the crime rate in our communities and the rise in violence and hate amongst one another, with most of the dialogue being targeted toward the lack of jobs, racial profiling by police, the lack of opportunity and safe havens, or some other outside influence. Which all play a part in the crime rates we've experienced in the Black and brown communities, don't get me wrong; but a more important conversation has to start from within. We are reaping what we have sown, when we see young black men robbing, stealing, and killing one another. They are completing the agenda of those that came before them, a by product of poor parenting, influence of drugs and alcohol, dysfunctional relationships and unhealthy marriages, lack of discipline and disobedience to God. Young girls flaunting their bodies and lack value because some of them have not been taught what it means to be modest, to have self respect and love. We have flaunted the lifestyle of quick money, flashy cards, and material possessions so they find refuge in the name brand belts and purses, crackin' credit cards, stealing identities, and getting surgery enhancements to be something they're not. It's true, we have not sat around having real conversation with our youth about the importance of abstaining from sex before marriage, and how soul ties with someone you don't know may cause you to pick up the behaviors and spiritual battles of someone else, becoming lustful, full of envy and insecure, bi-polar and depressed. We have not celebrated the smart kids who believe in themselves, willing to stand out and be different, be a trendsetter and not fall into peer pressure to do what others are doing even if it harms them. The cool kids have become the pill poppin, pants hanging, hair weave killas, similar to the generation before. There is no new thing under the sun, so we are reaping the harvest of wicked behavior, misunderstood trauma filled young adults who have yet to find Jesus and yet to find themselves. While the rest of us on the other hand, are raising our children in wisdom of the True and Living God, teaching them scripture, showing them positive ways to build wealth, helping them build faith and courage to shine in dark places, dare to be different and not be apologetic about wanting more. They are learning to be an asset, to bring value to the table, and have a life devoted to walking in the Will of God. And though we have not always lived this way, we have repented of our sins and turned our lives over to the one who created us. When you do good, good comes back to you, but when you indulge in sin and evil that too comes back around. Sometimes even cursing the children we bare and the next generation causing them to suffer and repeat, like Now. Millennials and Gen Y generations are just the product of open wounds and destruction that our parents refused to handle. Some of us are the bleeding wounds that were buried in molestation, birth out of covenant, children of addiction, faithless prayers, working to make ends meet and never striving for more, imprisoned bodies and minds, inherited debt, and pride. We have to collectively humble ourselves and be better sowers, healers, warriors, and children of the Most High. The world is dependent on us!

Galatians 6:7-9 says Be not deceived; God is not mocked: for whatsoever a man soweth, that shall he also reap. For he that soweth to his flesh shall of the flesh reap corruption; but he that soweth to the Spirit shall of the Spirit reap life everlasting. And let us not be weary in well doing: for in due season we shall reap, if we faint not.

****Self Reflection: What are you reaping?
What have you sown?**

_____

_____

_____

_____

_____

_____

_____

_____

_____

_____

When Two Walk in Agreement

Blessings to My Kings & Queens

Proverbs 15:1 says, "A soft answer turns away wrath, but a harsh word stirs up anger." It is better to handle disagreement amongst two, than to fight and bicker or cause strife. Being in agreement with someone is extremely important and most times necessary in order for the relationship or friendship to blossom. And healthy conflict amongst people can be handled with respect and dignity without screaming, blame shifting, or name calling. Trust me, this was an area I had to learn real fast. Growing up, there were a lot of times I got my way and it didn't require a lot of compromise. Well as I got older, and start experiencing push back from other people, I was shocked, like "wait a minute, I'm not used to this." It's my way or the highway, so what it's gone be. I wasn't looking for a happy medium, I just needed for that person, regardless if it were in friendships or relationships, I need you to agree with me. Well, that didn't work and I was eventually brought to a place that truly humbled me, and broke my ego down. Through a series of encounters, I learned to compromise and seek the best for others, I had been disrespected and hurt in a way that made me mute for some time. I had lost the ability to stand up for myself and I realized after the fact, that Yah was showing me that is how I made others feel. The Lord was teaching me to be compassionate and considerate of others, He taught me to think highly of others and not let my light dim in the presence of someone else. I didn't have to be right to be recognized, I din't have to know it all, I didn't have to prove anything to others; but I did have to help them find their voice the way I found mine. Because hurt people, hurt people and we do not always make the best decisions in learning the simple ways of communication as written in the word of God. When we have agreement, there is harmony, there is unity, there is a sense of togetherness and we can accomplish so much more. We can listen to others and hear them out, we can have a meeting of the mind and share ideas, no one person is greater than the other, and we can attack as problem without attacking each other. The same way we express patience and resilience with ourselves, we should lend that same love and self-control with someone else. Matthew 18:15 says "If your brother sins against you, go and tell him his fault, between you and him alone. If he listens to you, you have gained your brother." That is going in confidence to your brother or sister, we don't have to broadcast our frustrations to other people who will then speak negative or garner some type of feelings toward the person too. We have to share in honesty, understanding, and forgiveness in a conversation of disagreement. And if done right, this method can be used with siblings, spouses, friends, coworkers, or anyone out of agreement. But if the situation cannot be mended or repaired, simply walk away with a clean heart, as to not harbor those emotions for what did not work out. Sometimes things are just not meant to be, and we have to be content in knowing that.

Amos 3:3 "Can two walk together, except they be agreed?"

Matthew 18:19 "Again I say unto you, That if two of you shall agree on Earth as touching anything that they shall ask, it shall be done for them of my Father which is in heaven."

**Self Reflection: What area of your life lack agreement?

___

Stubborn Prayers

Blessings to My Kings & Queens

Have you ever prayed for something, really hard and I mean daily prayer; asking Yah to bless you with something or someone, crying out to Him, and desperately wanting it. Then all of a sudden, you get exactly what you pray for, and things aren't what you expected them to be. So now your praise report has become another problem, the very thing you were praying for comes with persecution, hard work, frustration, test and trial. When we seek Yah to answer prayers, most times it is to fix a problem or resolve an issue of the heart, so we don't foresee the obstacles we'll endure to maintain it. For instance, have you ever dealt with crazy amounts of debt, tired of robbing Peter to pay Paul, living paycheck to paycheck barely making ends meet. And you begin to pray for breakthrough, asking Yah to bless you with promotion, financial increase; hoping that He will make a way. Well He answers your prayer and sure enough the promotion comes with a tough team to work with, people who cause friction and confusion, more responsibilities for you, and it just seems like none of it is worth the increase. Now the prayer has been answered, you're able to pay bills and relieve some stress in that area, only asking Yah for the basic necessities of your need, but have caused persecution in another area of your life. He never said that we won't have trouble, He never said we won't experience trial and persecution to build character, He never said that His provisions will come without responsibility. But this is where the understanding of too whom much is given, much is required.

Romans 12:12 says "Be joyful in hope, patient in affliction, and faithful in prayer."

This scripture explains how important it is to Be joyful in the things we hope for and learn to understand the affliction that comes with it. Just because we got what we prayed for doesn't mean it won't require work, time, and energy; as a matter of fact, this is the time when Yah requires more faith, more obedience, more pressure, to be a good steward over His blessings. Be grateful for that which you have and understand whatever you desire and ask of Him, you'll be expected to have power and dominion in that area; just like Jesus, He expects you to be a good Shepherd over the family, a good Shepherd over the business, a good Shepherd over the neighborhood. That's why the word says, Be careful for what you pray for...cause things are not always what it seem. Don't be like Abraham and pray for a son, and when it doesn't happen the way you want it to, you take things in your own hand. Don't ask Yah for a blessing or healing and then not expect the labor and works of your hand to increase too. The Lord said I will bless you as I see fit. Your inheritance will be through the nation I said. Some of us are complaining about the very thing we prayed for. Lord help us maintain and be good stewards of your blessings.

**Self Reflection: Prayer

Heavenly Father, I thank you for answering my prayers, I thank you for the agreement of your Word and turning things around in my favor. I thank you for inclining you ear to me and healing my loved one, I thank you for getting me out of that abusive relationship, Lord I thank you for healing my broken heart and relieving the Spirit of depression. Lord I thank you for gifting me with vision and endurance, for blessing me with great ideas and profitable work to build generational wealth. I thank you for making me the lender and not the borrower, I thank you for removing the Spirit of peer pressure and rebuking the Spirit of cowardice, making me strong and bold in you. Lord I thank you for the family you have blessed me with and answering the prayers of my husband and I, allowing us to conceive and have a beautiful family. Oh God I thank you for teaching me to be a good steward over my finances and training me up to be a millionaire and defy the odds of my community, for giving me wisdom, knowledge, and understanding to give back and train up another generation. I thank you for removing the taste of addiction out of my mouth and allowing me to go back and share my testimony with other men and women struggling in that area. The work is hard, the persecution and affliction is heavy, but I am a co-worker with you, and your Glory shall reign through me.

In Jesus name Amen

What Have you Prayed For and Have not Been Grateful?

_____

_____

_____

_____

_____

_____

_____

_____

_____

_____

_____

Busy Doin' Nothing

Blessings to My Kings & Queens

One of the most dangerous and nonconstructive moves we can make is sit around in idleness, a group of individuals doing nothing, having frivolous conversation, and ego tripping dialogue. This is the foundation of so many disagreements amongst friends, I can remember last year when everyone was discussing the hot topic of Stephen Curry and Ayesha Curry on the Red Table talk with Jada Pinkett-Smith. Some people agreed with Ayesha's approach of speaking on the truth of her marriage and some experiences they had, while others were upset with her willingness to air "dirty laundry" or share her stance on the nature of her relationship. It became a debate amongst men and women, a debate in barbershop talk, a debate at the nail salon, and even the radio shows chimed in. Everyone was talking about it, and it caused friction in some circles because they couldn't agree to disagree, people wanted their point to be heard, yelling and screaming across the tables, relationships in jeopardy due to personal lives of celebrities they didn't even know. I've seen friendships torn apart, I've seen fights break out from individuals who sat around gossiping and speaking on things that had nothing to do with them. Nonconstructive speech does not help us move forward, it does not create opportunity or build closeness, it repeats a cycle of dead weight; causing division, strife, and negativity. We have to Be careful not to sit around in idleness having unproductive, negative conversations…it kills the vibe. The vibe of peace, joy, and calmness. It begins in innocent gossip about nonsense or small talk, and eventually grow and fester into slander, spewing words of hate and division toward one another, name calling and speaking ill, wishing bad on someone and eventually preying on their downfall. This happens because misery loves company, and eventually wear out its welcome, especially in moments of unintentional link-ups (hangouts).

1 Timothy 5:13
"Besides that, they learn to be idlers, going about from house to house, and not only idlers, but also gossips and busybodies, saying what they should not."

Proverbs 16:27-29
"Idle hands are the devil's workshop; idle lips are his mouthpiece. An evil man sows strife; gossip separates the best of friends."

**Self Reflection: How can I be intentional about my time with others; card parties, barbershop talk, beauty shop gossip, kitchen table discussion, phone conversations, petty talk?

_____

_____

_____

_____

_____

Plan to Fail or Fail to Plan

Blessings to My Kings & Queens

Sometimes the reason things don't happen or opportunities don't come our way, is because we don't prepare for them. It's not that we're being looked over or counted out, but it's simply because we don't grasp what's right there in front of us. I've come to realize that life is not about wandering, and stumbling upon blessings or opened doors of opportunity; but its about being strategic planning, purpose, and intention. Don't spend your life wandering and falling into traps of uncertainty, but explore the Earth, set a plan, and fill your backpack for the adventure, just like Dora the Explorer. Dora had a backpack full of items that she will need to go over each hurdle, she knew what route to take, and when she came across a fox ready to steal, kill and destroy; she had a friend to help her defeat his schemes.   Habbakuk 2:2 says, Then the LORD answered me and said, "Record the vision And inscribe it on tablets, That the one who reads it may run." Write down your visions and aspirations, make it plain and stay focused, and though it may take time to come to pass, you'll have reason to fight through the struggle and disappointment. Give yourself something to work towards and though it may tarry, Yah will still give provision and manifest that which is desired. See Yah wants to see our faith at work, He wants to know that we have a plan and work towards accomplishing those goals; going to school, graduating and getting our degree, starting a business and being successful at it, investing into properties and building a brand, training hard and getting drafted to the league, purchasing a home and having a successful marriage, writing the play and producing the film, opening the shelter and starting the organization, whatever it is, whatever you believe, write it down. Because the truth is even if you aim for the moon, at least you'll land amongst the stars. We are a great and mighty people, and sometimes we forget the ancient landmarks that have been placed before us. But truth is, we'd be better off as a people if we study our ancestors and the success of their plight in history. Those were the plans of our nation, and if we expound on them, replicate them, and build upon them; we'll go further and reach higher than we've ever done before. Look at the works of the Talented tenth and W.E.B. Dubois, look at the agenda of Marcus Garvey and the Black Panther 10 point strategy, look at the work ethic of Madam C J Walker, look at the uprise in black businesses of Tulsa, Chicago, and Detroit, look at the Harlem Renaissance era, and association of Black institutions. Our history is rich, our history is prosperous, and our history is proof of Yah's covenant with Israel. Study these plans, understand these blueprints, and locate your lane to dominate.

Proverbs 21:15
"The plans of the diligent lead surely to abundance, but everyone who is hasty comes only to poverty."

Luke 14:28
"For which of you, desiring to build a tower, does not first sit down and count the cost, whether he has enough to complete it?"

Proverbs 16:3
"Commit your work to the Lord, and your plans will be established."

Self Reflection: Create a Vision Board, what are your goals, what do you want to accomplish?

_____

_____

_____

_____

_____

_____

_____

_____

_____

_____

_____

_____

_____

Power of Waiting

Blessings to My Kings & Queens

Have you ever considered the Power of waiting on a Train. I know, I know…it can be one of the most frustrating times ever, getting caught by a freight train when you were on your way somewhere, and literally have to sit through the slow, drag of watching each cart. Cars in front of you are turning around because they refuse to wait any longer, cars behind you are backing up and going in the opposite direction. And here you are, making the decision to wait until it clears, you're not looking for another route, checking to see how much longer it'll be, and making u-turns to go elsewhere. We have to learn the concept of being still, and knowing that this too shall pass. Sometimes things are not gonna happen when we want them too, sometimes there will be roadblocks and barriers in our way that won't require us to fight, fumble, or faint. But instead wait patiently on the Lord to move on our behalf, He may be forcing us to wait for a reason. And building up the muscle to remain focused, not grow weary and restless, helps us to stand firm on the righteousness of God. Isaiah 40:31 says " But they that wait upon the Lord shall renew their strength; they shall mount up with wings as eagles; they shall run, and not be weary; and they shall walk, and not faint." Be patient in this season and study for preparation on what's to come. Practice your ability to say No, trust God for what He said He will do, and during your waiting period Be still. This is the time God speaks the most, He wants your undivided attention, He wants your surrendered heart, He wants your busy schedule, He wants your pride and joy, He wants your commitment and devotion. So don't panic when things seem to take longer, don't fret when it appears like what He promised cannot happen in the place you're in, and don't doubt the route He has given you to see it manifest. This waiting period will give you time to heal some old wounds, it'll give you time to position your thoughts and beliefs on Him, it'll strengthen your prayer life, and allow you to have a deeper relationship with God. Life is happening to all of us, and we can get distracted by the movement of others, and begin to follow suit if we've been waiting; but God is showing us that He has hand upon us, preparing that spouse, opening those lanes, revealing your name, and providing your space. It is so!

Lamentations 3:25
"The Lord is good to those who wait for him, to the soul who seeks him."

James 5:7-8
"Be patient, therefore, brothers, until the coming of the Lord. See how the farmer waits for the precious fruit of the earth, being patient about it, until it receives the early and the late rains. You also, be patient. Establish your hearts, for the coming of the Lord is at hand."

Psalm 37:7
"Be still before the Lord and wait patiently for him; fret not yourself over the one who prospers in his way, over the man who carries out evil devices!"

**Self Reflection: What Has the Lord told you to wait on?

_____
_____
_____
_____
_____
_____
_____
_____
_____
_____
_____
_____
_____
_____
_____

Too Many Options, Now what

Blessings to My Kings & Queens

So I was having a conversation with Yah one day, as I often times do. Our relationship is tight like that, He's not only Jehovah Jireh (my provider) but He's also the Author and Finisher of my Faith, He's my Abba (Father), and my Big Homie. We have a close relationship, and because of my maturity in Him, I've learned to consider Him in ALL things. So anyway I was driving one day and was talking to the Lord about a things He had promised me, and revealed to me that I should be working on. And I was like Bro' I don't know why you want me to do that, in such a oversaturated lane, like how you gone call me to do this and it's like so many people already doing it. Lord I thought we had other plans remember, what about when you told me as a little girl to motivate people, to inspire them to live out their dreams. What about the trips to the Women Shelters at 13, where you ignited in me to give back, to educate women on abuse and addiction, what about the plans to create job opportunities for others and the books you had me writing at 14 years old. Life happened Lord, and I don't know if I still have it in me to go back to that place. Everyone is doing it, you want me to post stuff, you know I don't mess with social media, you want me to share my story and go back to ideas you had me write down and work on years ago. Wowwww… okay but I'm just saying, Lord you see errbody and they mama doing this. I don't move like that and you know it, I like to be in my own lane, I like to move different, some of these visions that will come to pass, will catch everybody off guard, you sure. And Yah start speaking to me like girl hush. "Do you hear yourself, remember what I told you before you graduated from high school, remember what I showed you at 13, remember what I shared with you and made you write down years ago, I plan on manifesting ALL of those things. I set you apart, I called you out, I created you for a time as this. Think about the bread aisle, there are hundreds of brands, selling the same product, do you think they care, has it stopped their overflow? I am who I am, and I know the numbers of hairs on your head. We are doing this together, and I don't care how many options there are, YOU are needed." See the conversation I was having with my Father was a reminder to keep working, stay the course and complete the task; because even though it looks overcrowded, my lane is clear, and it is designed for me. I want you to consider that same philosophy for your own life, you are fearfully and wonderfully made; and God does not discount what He has called you to do, so regardless if it seems someone else is already doing it, know that His plan for you is tailor made.

Matthew 22:14
"For many are called, but few are chosen."

John 15:16
"You did not choose me, but I chose you and appointed you that you should go and bear fruit and that your fruit should abide, so that whatever you ask the Father in my name, he may give it to you."

**Self Reflection: What Has Yah called you to Do?

_____

_____

_____

_____

_____

_____

_____

_____

_____

_____

_____

_____

_____

_____

_____

_____

Spirit of Jealousy

Blessings to My Kings and Queens:

One of the first things we learn as believers and studying the Word, the Holy Bible; is that God's wrath and anger toward us came from Jealousy. God was jealous and upset that His children were disobedient to His laws, statutes, and commandments. There was a time when our ancestors refused to obey God's word and live our life in obedience to His Torah and caused us to be placed in bondage. A time when His sons and daughters were full of sin and participating in idolatry, envy, pride, promiscuity, fornication, and deceit. Our treacherous behavior was deemed as unrighteousness, and caused pain and fiery to a Heavenly Father who loves us so much. Can you imagine hurting one of your parents because of bad behavior and your unwillingness to do what they asked of you, especially when they know what's best. How many times have we thanked our parents for providing, and keeping a roof over our head? How many times have we thanked our parents for coming to save us when we got ourselves in trouble? And how many times have we given them the credit for loving us and pouring confidence in us even when we didn't see fit to love ourselves. Well this is the angle of Jealousy our Father in Heaven has for us.

Unlike the Jealousy we display toward one another, God's envy is full of compassion, loving kindness, and protection. We instead invoke bitterness and selfish deceit toward our sisters and brothers in the Spirit of the enemy. Comparing ourselves to what others have, gossiping when they've been promoted, coveting over someone else's relationship and marriage even when you only see the Highlight reel. We carry this sense of ungratefulness for the things God has done for us when we discredit them in comparison. There is a reason and a season for everything under the sun, and I pray that you learn to trust God's timing and find enjoyment in the blessings bestowed upon you from the Most High. For there are things that another may have, and you're praying to God for, but do not understand the assignment in which they have been given. Your purpose may call for a spouse that works in a field similar to yours as you build the company, your life may call for you to adopt a child to prove your ability to love without limits, your life may call for you to experience humble beginnings to build character and not pride as you elevate higher. So be careful not to dwell in the Spirit of Jealousy and be consumed with anger and selfish intent; for it has not been revealed what the Lord has planned for you. Don't let your blessings pass you by, because you fail to acknowledge the goodness of where you are in this season. Your Grace for Growth is on the way! And God just require you to be in position to receive, that which He has already promised. No good thing will God withhold from you, nor will he forsake you.

James 3:14-15 declares "But if you have bitter jealousy and selfish ambition in your hearts, do not boast and be false to the truth. This not the wisdom that comes down from above, but is earthly, unspiritual, and demonic.

**Self Reflection: Can you recall a time you've grown weary and jealous? How can your joy for others, prove to God that you're grateful for what He's doing and has already done?

_____

_____

_____

_____

_____

_____

_____

_____

_____

_____

_____

_____

_____

_____

He Paid the Price...You Live the Life

Blessings to My Kings & Queens

   One of my favorite scriptures is Romans 5:8, "but God shows his love for us in that while we were still sinners, Christ died for us." During a season in my life where I was unwilling to forgive myself, and didn't know where to begin, this scripture spoke to me. It gave me a level of freedom in Yahweh, that I had never thought was possible for me. After making so many mistakes, following the matters of my heart, and falling into trap after trap of self inflicted pain; I realized that grace was available to me, mercy was being extended to me, because yet while I was a sinner, Christ died for me. This may sound a bit cliché, but after being scolded in church and being told by my elders, "if you do this you're going to hell, if you do that you're going to hell, keep living like a heathen and you'll be dead with gasoline draws on." Well the first time I sinned, I was too young to know the magnitude of those sins, I didn't know what I was doing and thought, I was "just making mistakes" like every child does. And if there is no forgiveness and the deed is already done, and I'm going to hell anyway, why would I stop now. See, some of us have been taught of Yah, by the Pharisee doctrine, we've been condemned by our past mistakes and judged by our iniquities. Now don't get me wrong, we'll have to answer to these things one day and make an account of our wrongdoings, but Yah has appointed that time, not the saints around us. Thus we have been extended a grace period, a season to repent of our sins and ask for forgiveness, we've received the Blood of Jesus to wash us clean and reconcile us with our Lord and Saviour. So I am not the accumulation of my past mistakes, I am more than the girl who grew up smoking and drinking, fighting and fornicating, playing wife in an unhealthy relationship, searching for love in all the wrong places, lost my identity in the streets, and became a single mom forced to raise my son with extended support from his dad. I fought hard for my relationship, I wanted things to work and gave more of me to everybody around me, and left nothing for self. I lost my cousin to the streets during a time we both fell on our faces to Yah and start devoting ourselves back to church. I blamed myself for not being there for her and went into a deep depression, I buried all of my pain and began to wear a mask, covering up the blemishes of insecurity, anger, selfishness, fear, and doubt of who I was. How did Yah allow things to go so far, and I not even recognize who I was anymore. My heart was bleeding and there was no pain pill, no bottle of Remy, no sexual addiction, no party, no amount of money, and nobody who could HEAL me the way Jesus could. So I began seeking Him again, a personal walk in the wilderness, being tempted by the devil over and over and over again. But I confessed my sins, I revealed myself to Yah, and I shared my hurt and pain; knowing that if He wanted to, He could turn all of those things around for me. And He did, yet while I was sinning, He died for me; proving that His will for my life is greater than my circumstances, and if I would just humble myself, He would do a new thing. I went through a strenuous process, of studying and learning to hear Yah's voice, I spoke with Him daily and began to feed my mind with daily affirmations of His word. I switched up my circle, I changed my appetite, I no longer yearned the things that didn't please Him, and began to fast more and cause my mind to be in obedience, I denied myself of sex and vowed to wait until marriage. Truth is, I went through the wilderness with the Armor of God on, changing my language, finding my purpose, learning my gifts, and allowing the Holy Spirit to lead. I accepted righteousness, I learned who the true and living God is, I studied my ancestors the real Israelites, I found my Hebrew heritage, the real Jews; who were scattered abroad during the Middle Passage of Slavery for our disobedience. I found favor in His sight, and replaced the name of idols, I found refuge and glory in the books of the Bible that were removed, that spoke to our true identity as Kings and Queens, I gained my confidence back, and was made whole again. You too can experience this Freedom, You too can accept Yahuah Hamashiach (Jesus Christ) as your Lord and Saviour, because I am a Living Testimony of His Grace and Promises. Nothing you did was a surprise to Yah, and those life challenges were already created to birth the warrior in you.

Why are People so Afraid of the S word….

Blessings to My Kings & Queens

There is so much dialogue and disagreement around the conversation of Submission. Men say one thing and women say another, some believe in submission and others don't. It is such a touchy subject, that it is often glossed over in fear that it strikes a cord with the wrong crowd. Well truth is, I believe it is also denied its proper attention because of misunderstanding, we refuse to talk about that which we are unfamiliar. For some odd reason, Submission is equated to weakness and no one wants to seem or be viewed as weak. Let me grab my vest before the arrows start blazing, welp I hate to tell you but, SUBMISSION is not weakness, but instead it is STRENGTH. The ability to accept, agree, and surrender to the assignment or mission of someone else is submission. You have to be strong, confident, and sure of yourself to come in alignment with Yah's will for the good of those around you or your spouse. Not sure why we have such a hard time doing this in marriage, but have time and time again, complied and submitted to the position of a job, school, social organization, and even Satan's schemes. Some of us have applied and accepted jobs without even reading the mission statement of the company, not knowing what we're signing up for as long as it pays well. Some have even joined bike clubs, car clubs, gangs, fraternities and sororities, tv subscriptions, urban league groups, and other organizations without ever considering what they stand for, how do they impact the community, what our involvement entail, does this edify Yah's kingdom, and what does this mean for me. While others, accept the plots and schemes of people we run with, look for ways to connive and trick others, find a slick way to move within the institutions of government, and link up with like minded spirits that share the same agenda. And here we are complaining about submitting to the purpose and vision of our spouse, even though we VOWED to love them for better or for worse, be with them through sickness and in health, support them for richer or for poorer; which all sounds like an act of submission to me. There is strength and power in the unity of submitting to a plan, acceptance and agreement before Yah to see those visions come to pass. Husbands submit yourselves to loving your wife, covering and protecting her, being diligent about your works to provide for her and the children, to consider your decisions and the impact it has on the family; just as Christ did for the church. Wives submit to the leadership of your husband, trusting that He is led by the Father and has been given charge with your support, insight, and expertise to build generational wealth, successfully raise a family, and contribute to helping others grow. Both of you have an integral role in expanding the kingdom and advancing our people in godliness. It is not about control, selfishness, and possessive behavior; it does not wage war on each other, or intimidate character, but instead reveal true love and harmony when two are in agreement. This is the power of Submission!

Ephesians 5:21
" Submit to one another out of reverence for Christ. Wives, submit yourselves to your own husbands as you do to the Lord. For the husband is the head of the wife as Christ is the head of the church, his body, of which he is the Savior. Now as the church submits to Christ, so also wives should submit to their husbands in everything. Husbands, love your wives, just as Christ loved the church and gave himself up for her."

Job 22:21
"Submit to God and be at peace with him; in this way prosperity will come to you."

James 4:7
"Submit yourselves, then, to God. Resist the devil, and he will flee from you."

**Self Reflection: What are your fears regarding Submission?

_____
_____
_____
_____
_____
_____
_____
_____
_____
_____

Supernatural Power

Blessings to My Kings & Queens

Remember Mary was a humble virgin from Nazareth, in preparation to marry Joseph, who had no intent of giving birth to the Messiah. And though she gladly accepted the assignment of the Lord when the angel came to her, she probably would have had apprehension, had she known the crucifixion would come. But God qualifies us for the assignment and will of His kingdom. We cannot always see how things would come to pass, or know how they would turn out when God gives us a task that seem impossible to perform. Here we are with limited thinking and resources, asking God, how could it be? Think about the characters below, and consider how they accomplished so much with the Supernatural Power given.

Peter Parker became Spiderman
Clark Kent became Superman
Jacob became Israel
Abram became Abraham
Nipsey Hussle returned to Ermias
Detroit Red became Malcolm X

Expect a name change in this next season and know that Yah will use the anointing, the oil that He placed upon you in the womb of your mother to accelerate and propel you to new heights. We all have a supernatural gift that was designed to be used in the BODY of Christ, we are different members of the same body and when we come to understand that, we are less likely to separate ourselves from the body to serve just us and not others. We can then stop using our gifts and talents for our own personal gain, and instead experience the overflow and joy we receive by allowing Yah to use our gifts for His Glory. Some of us have not realized how our voice heal others, some of us are not aware that our compassion for others break chains, some of us do not know our ability to test Spirits break strongholds, and most of us have become so mute, that we don't realize our testimonies have saved lives. Use your super power, study your gifts and anointing, seek wisdom and ask Yah to create opportunities of light so that you shine in dark places. You'll step into your greatness and be transformed forever, the Old you will not recognize the New and Improved version; and that's only because you'll have a new Name. Let me introduce myself, I am Zion..a daughter of Yahweh the Most High, I am called to lead many nations back to the True and Living Elohim. I am a queen, a royal priesthood, assigned to serve one of many mansions in my Father's house. To live a life of abundance and peace, to share His goodness and walk in truth, I live, I love, and I draw from streams of living water. My fruit produce a good return and give access to the flock to glean and eat for generations to come. I build wealth, I restore healthy marriages, and I help groom godly men and women, I dispel myths, I break chains, and cast down strongholds with the help of Heaven's angels. I speak life, I promote freedom, and I enlarge territory for the sake of My Father's name…all through the works of my Brother Yeshua Hamashiach (Jesus Christ).

Acts 14:3
"So they remained for a long time, speaking boldly for the Lord, who bore witness to the word of his grace, granting signs and wonders to be done by their hands."

1 John 2:20

"But you have an anointing from the Holy One, and you all know."

**Self Reflection: Lord I give you my gifts to be used for your Glory and I command your Supernatural Power to fall Afresh on Me.

_____

_____

_____

_____

_____

_____

_____

www.ingramcontent.com/pod-product-compliance
Lightning Source LLC
Chambersburg PA
CBHW071346080526
44587CB00017B/2982